making music in looking glass land

FOURTH EDITION

A Guide to Survival
and Business Skills for
the Classical Musician

Ellen Highstein
with additional research and text by Oliver Brewer

concertartistsguild

Highstein, Ellen.
with additional research and text by Oliver Brewer

Making Music in Looking Glass Land:
A Guide to Survival and Business Skills for the Classical Musician.

ISBN 1-892862-05-0

Concert Artists Guild is a non-profit organization which, since its founding in 1951, has been dedicated to identify, nurture and support the careers of gifted young classical musicians. For further information on CAG programs, visit us on the Web at www.concertartists.org.

Contents

Introduction   3

Who should find this book useful?
What this book includes, and what it doesn't
A note for composers
How is this book organized?
Acknowledgments
A Note to the Fourth Edition

I.   The Lay of the Land   8

The Marketplace
The Customer
Self-knowledge (Musically Speaking)
Specifics

II.   Written and Visual Materials   15

Biographies
Photographs
The Press Kit
Flyers
Concert Flyers

III. Making a Recording   60

Sources of Materials
      • Labeling
      • A Word About Video
Setting up a professional recording session
      • Finding a Room
      • Finding an Engineer
      • On the Technical Side of Things
      • Using a Producer
      • Editing
      • In the Studio
Costs
      • Some Tips to Keep Costs Down
      • Making a Recording on a Small Budget
Distributing Your CD
      • The Major-Label Industry as It Stands Now
      • The Future of Selling Recordings
      • Marketing Your CD
      • The Internet and Recordings

IV.   Creating a Presence on the Internet   73

Why have a web page?
Deciding what your website should be
Putting it together
      • Creating a web page
      • Important elements of a website

V.   Assembling Credentials   78

Competitions
- Where are they? What are they?
- Which competitions to enter
- Choosing repertoire
- If you don't win
- When you win

Debuts … and Alternatives
- New York debut alternatives
- About Recital Managers

VI.   Networking   96

Patrons
- Know Your Customer
- How do you Start? Specifics of Making Requests
- Sample request letters
- Guidelines for individual fund-raising

Conductors

Composers … from the performer's perspective

VII.   The Press and Public Relations   123

Newspapers
- The Press Release
- The Pitch Letter
- Sending Your Materials
- The Print Press: Beyond Your Own Daily Papers

The Electronic Media
- Radio
- Being interviewed
- Getting Other Radio Publicity Free
- Television

Press Lists

The Public Relations Campaign

VIII. Management and Self-Management   147

Management
- What are managers looking for?
- How do I know that I'm ready for management?
- How do I get a manager?
- Which management is right for me?
- How much does management cost?
- What am I responsible for … ?

Alternatives to Major Management
- Medium Size and Smaller Management Firms
- Artist-run Group Managements

Self-Management
- Booking a date in four not-very-easy steps
- What to do if you've got the date
- Some general guidelines
- Sample Artist/Presenter Contract

IX.   All of the Above: For Composers   181

Performing and composing
Not performing … but out in the field
What about teaching?
Developing skills and learning about the field early on
Even if it's not too early … Some general advice
Working with performers
Sending scores and CDs to performers
Publishers
- From the composer's point of view
- Self publishing …

Other important skills for composers
Materials

X.   Fine Tuning   210

For Singers
Pianists: Work after graduation
Teaching and Performing

XI. On Stage   219

XII. Summing Up   226

It's never too early to ...
What not to leave school without
Is this all there is?
The Artist's Responsibility

XIII. General Resources   234

Non-Profit Status
Individual Artists Assistance
Unions and Professional Associations
Some Final Resource Suggestions: Survival
Day Jobs

Introduction

Concert Artists Guild produced annual career development workshops between 1983 and 1996. Called *Career Moves*, the workshops were a way of being useful to a larger, constituency than would be possible by working only with the entrants to and winners of CAG's annual New York Competition.

It seemed to those at CAG that most musicians, when they emerge from conservatory, are unprepared for the demands they face in the professional world. Though most pre-professional training may be less than adequate in regard to the realities of post-graduation life, musicians face an additional handicap, which is, perhaps, unique; they are encouraged, in preparing for a life in music, to specifically avoid thinking about anything but art . . . or technique, of course. Most performers begin to study music when they are extremely young, and are enthusiastically, sometimes lavishly, rewarded for their talent and effort. Until they graduate into the professional arena, the message is, "just keep practicing; your talent is all you need." When reality hits, they find out that it's not all they need, by a long shot. The effect of meeting the field as it is - moving from a world where everyone knows and respects you to one in which no one knows you, or seems to care much - can be daunting, even devastating. Some kind of orientation, addressing subjects rarely covered in the university or conservatory music curriculum, seemed to be badly needed.

The workshops featured speakers who could represent a point of view rarely discussed at music school: that of the "consumer," the people hiring, managing or otherwise representing artists, as well as those who make up their audiences. We also presented the artists themselves, who, having been through it all had definite points of view about what works and what doesn't. This book was written to make the valuable insights of all those speakers available to a broader public.

Since it's original publication, the role of this book has changed; many conservatories and universities now offer courses in career skills, or provide at least some of this information in more informal ways. The book has now become a text for such courses, and a self-help guide for those who don't have access to them.

In part because of this, in this edition of "Making Music" we've chosen to eliminate the Resource Sections that followed each chapter in previous versions. The book is now most frequently used in a context in which teachers or counselors can provide useful, up-to-date information. Experience showed us that the information provided in our Resource Sections was often outdated before the book was in general circulation, and was also geographically limited due to our inability to provide specific information beyond New York and a very few other places. However, we have still included the most general references which should remain useful to the aspiring musician for the forseeable future.

Those of us at CAG believe that there is inestimable value in studying and making music, that highly trained, gifted musicians should be able to survive to work in their field, and that they shouldn't be stopped in this effort by not knowing how to keep afloat.

To survive in a difficult environment requires knowledge and creativity, no less in this field than elsewhere. By encouraging artists to become informed about the field and their possible place in it, we seek to broaden their knowledge; by shaking up the artists' viewpoints, and getting them to look at the world through other eyes, we hope to stimulate their creativity.

We believe that it is not harmful to musicians to think about issues not directly related to how they play, sing, compose. *But we also believe they usually don't think enough even about how they do all these things, in the larger sense - that is, whether they're making music in a way which adds a new thought and a new voice to the field.* They also may not have considered whether there will be audiences who will hear them. Therefore, included in the book is a chapter on the artists' relationship to and responsibility for the future of the field – which is, in the end, the most important factor of all in career success: that is, helping to insure that there will be a field in which to be successful!

Who should find this book useful?

This book is aimed most directly at emerging, professional-level performers and composers of classical music. It often concentrates on specific issues faced by artists aspiring to careers as soloists or chamber musicians, or artists who wish to make solo or chamber music performance part of their professional lives. However, because it includes information that could be described as Business For Musicians 101, it should be useful to anyone trying to break into the music field - or perhaps other fields as well. Switching the focus to another venture within the profession requires some common sense substitutions of names, categories, and the like, but the concepts remain the same.

What this book includes, and what it doesn't

We've chosen here to address topics which are both basic to an understanding of how the field works and which are the ones about which musicians most consistently seem to want information. It would be impossible to convey the breadth of knowledge and wealth of detail (not to mention the anecdotes and entertainment) provided by the expert and generous speakers who participated in the workshops; however, we've tried to maintain the tone of the workshops, which we hope was savvy without being cynical.

This is a how-to-survive-as-a-musician book, not a how-to-become-something-else book. It is neither professional training in publicity, audio engineering, graphic design, or anything else, nor is it vocational guidance if your efforts in career building don't succeed. We tell you how to write certain kinds of letters, and how to make some phone calls; however, when we deal with areas that require specific, non-musical technical skill in support of your career efforts, we suggest what you should aim for, how to spot problems and find solutions on a budget, and how to find a professional who will give you value for your money. Should you decide that you want to engineer your own tapes and CDs, produce your own graphics, or do the legal work involved in not-for-profit incorporation, there are other sources, far more complete than we could be here, which will tell you how. As for career alternatives, and day jobs, we've limited ourselves to references to other sources and some remarks interpolated into the text.

A note for composers

Composers' career development needs sometimes require a slightly different way of looking at the field and slightly different support materials. We hope that composers will read the whole book and not just the chapter on composers anyway, since our approach to developing a place in the field is basically the same for performers and for composers, and much of what is stated is therefore equally applicable to anyone in the business. It will require some patience, and some creative substitutions of terms or ideas as you go along. Our apologies for the resulting awkwardness, and our hope that you will find it worth the effort.

How is this book organized?

The order of the chapters very generally corresponds to the order of what is needed when in a developing career. That is, you probably will need a good recording and some decent pictures before you can approach those in the professional world; you may need to amass some credentials - through performances and competition experience for example - before approaching various important individuals who will form a supportive network of associates; you will need this network before you can approach a manager.

There are, however, many exceptions to this order. Chapter XI, "On Stage," should logically be at the beginning but appears near the end of the book, since it serves more as a reminder to take care of this issue rather than as advice and instruction on specifics. The second part of Chapter VIII (which deals with self management) could appear much earlier, perhaps in the section on developing credentials; it appears here to demonstrate how the gulf between management and self-management is more apparent than real. Also, the section on making CDs appears too early, in Chapter III; but it was simply easier to place this information in a section dealing with audio and recording.

Some ways of organizing all the preceding material appear in Chapter XII; here's where the reader will find sections entitled "It's Never Too Early To ..." and "What Not to Leave School Without," both of which should be helpful in personalizing your career development calendar.

Acknowledgments

This book is truly the product of the generosity and wisdom of the Career Moves workshop speakers, who participated in workshops between 1987 and 1996. CAG and I cannot sufficiently express our gratitude to them all.

The author owes a debt as well to all those who generously read, criticized, took apart and put together . . . and generally made great improvements to the third edition. They include, among others, Robert Besen, Mary Madigan, Christopher Crowley, and Sarah Schwartz. Robert Besen is due special, very grateful thanks, as an indefatigable original member of the workshop team, and as the provider of many ideas and much information.

A Note to the Fourth Edition

For this new edition of *Making Music*, several sections have been revised or added, sections have been deleted, and all the material has been extensively reviewed and rethought; nonetheless, some things have been left unchanged. When an example or an interview has been left unchanged from previous editions, it is probably because it still seemed to be the best example, or the most illuminating advice, that we could find.

For this edition, several sections were written by a gifted young musician, Oliver Brewer, who very successfully took on the challenge of writing about recordings and about the Internet, areas which have changed dramatically since the last edition. Additional help was provided by Brian Bumby and Elaine Sabino.

Ellen Highstein
former Executive Director
Concert Artists Guild
June 2003

I. The Lay of the Land

"Now! Now!" cried the Queen. "Faster! Faster!" And they went so fast that at last they seemed to skim through the air, hardly touching the ground with their feet till, suddenly, just as Alice was getting quite exhausted, they stopped, and she found herself sitting on the ground, breathless and giddy.

The Queen propped her up against a tree, and said kindly, "You may rest a little now."

Alice looked round her in great surprise. "Why, I do believe we've been under this tree the whole time! Everything's just as it was!"

"Of course it is," said the Queen. "What would you have it?"

"Well, in our country, " said Alice, still panting a little, "you'd generally get to somewhere else if you ran very fast for a long time, as we've been doing "

"A slow sort of country!" said the Queen. "Now, here, you see, it takes all the running you can do to keep in the same place. If you want to get somewhere else, you must run at least twice as fast as that!"

- Lewis Carroll, *Through the Looking Glass*

The field of classical music is, for most performers, like Looking Glass Land. There are a very few individuals who, because of circumstance - extreme youth combined with extraordinary ability, acknowledged elder statesman status, or an extra-musical and sensational entry into the field, for example - seem able to leave their career development problems to others: but they are very few and far between. For most musicians, the effort to stay in the same place, to keep working in the field, is constant and endless.

The performer is dependent for the success of this effort on the supportive assistance and good will of an exceptionally large group of people. He or she needs the enthusiasm, interest, confidence and familiarity of presenters, conductors, managers, the press, colleagues and audience. The classical music field is certainly not unique in this; other fields - politics for one - share in the fact that without the support of a large personal constituency one's career efforts are likely to fail. However, classical musicians are perhaps unique in believing the myth that great artistry, and more practicing, are all they need, and that having to go out and work on developing a constituency is proof of artistic failure.

In this fantasy the performer is encouraged by a system of training which, by and large, addresses only the question of how to sound good enough for the job rather than how to get the job. In fairness, since it is very difficult indeed to achieve great proficiency as a performer, the overwhelming amount of the conservatory's and the teacher's attention is necessarily directed to a restricted number of musical issues. Also, a few people seem naturally to have the creative instincts and political savvy which can win them admiration and employment. But working at developing these qualities is often seen within the field as detracting from the main business of playing, and the acquisition of them - if not discouraged - is generally not applauded.

Most musicians want to survive as musicians, though, and are willing to work to make that happen. It is impossible even with great effort and great talent, to guarantee a major career. Such careers exist as the result of a confluence of factors, many not under the control of either the performer or the performer's advisors. It is probably possible however, to make a career which allows the performer to keep making music before the public. It does take some changes in most musicians' thinking about the field and their role in it.

To maximize the chance of being in demand as a performer, you, the artist, must:

Know the marketplace

Understand who is listening to music, and when, where, why and how they're listening; who pays for the creation and performance of music, and how music and audiences are brought together; be able to see where flexibility exists in these market conditions, and how they can be influenced by a creative approach.

Know the customer

See the field from the consumer's point of view, including those of the various groups in your constituency.

Know yourself

Understand, specifically and precisely, what you have to contribute to the field, what makes you unique as a musician.

Acting on this knowledge does not imply changing to suit a current craze, or creating false relationships with those said to be important and influential. Rather, this understanding must be used to find your own supportive constituency, and to create opportunities for sharing your particular musical vision with others.

The Marketplace

It is important to understand that the field of classical music is a marketplace, with buyers and sellers, consumers and products. The consumers and buyers are a varied bunch, including audiences, concert presenters, musical colleagues (conductors, orchestra managers, artist managers and others), the press and electronic media and patrons. As in any marketplace, there is money being made and spent. Understanding where the money is, and what causes it to move around, is basic to understanding why the field functions as it does. As in any marketplace, there is at any given time more or less interest in a specific item. There are fashions and trends, caused by social, cultural, and economic factors.

It is a buyers' market. To demonstrate this in regard to performers, you need only attend one of the big performing arts trade shows, and see the market in action. Visiting the biggest of these, the annual conference sponsored by the Association of Performing Arts Presenters (APAP), can be an exceptionally unsettling (and perhaps discouraging) experience. Picture the enormous convention rooms of a major New York City hotel, filled with booths manned by managers and artists ranging from the giants (Columbia Artists Management and the like) to individual players. Music, dance, theater and everything else are cheek by jowl, vying for attention. With video monitors, photo and record displays, slogans, dishes of candy and free ice cream cones, the sellers try to attract the attention of the buyers: the concert presenters. Representatives of organizations presenting performers, from Lincoln Center to small arts series in tiny towns across the country, wander among the booths, looking for something new, something different - or perhaps not, perhaps looking for their friends, and for the same tried and true performances that have worked for them in the past.

The sellers outnumber the buyers. Each of the booths operated by a management represents a roster of artists; simple arithmetic is all that's needed to demonstrate how few opportunities there are relative to the number of artists who want them. Further divide the number of performance slots available by the number that feature music, and then by the few that want classical music. And then remember all those musicians not "on display," competing for the same jobs!

Other conditions have contributed to musicians' marketing difficulties. Among them is the fact that artists are often hired apart from direct experience of them as performers: on the basis of third party recommendations (from managers, critics, colleagues or teachers), or materials such as pictures, flyers and demo CDs. Furthermore, because of the current state of music education and the complexities of the way the field is administered, even when presenters have the opportunity to actually hear the artist in live performance, they may not be capable of or confident in their own ability to distinguish great from merely good, or even merely competent, music-making.

What all this means is, simply, too few jobs chased by too many good musicians. The artist must therefore define clear, realistic career goals in the field and understand what may be required, both musically and extra-musically, to achieve them.

The Customer

You need people to provide the support which will make it possible for you to work. Among them are:

Fans, audiences who will come to hear you (or hear your music, if you're a composer), pay for tickets, applaud, tell their friends, write to the concert presenter to get you rehired, and come again.

Presenters, people who will hire you to play.

Colleagues, other musicians or people in the field who will often be the primary source of direct employment or referrals for work, and who offer a network of musical and emotional support.

Patrons, individuals who have the wherewithal to provide financial or other support for career development when it's needed.

All of these consumers behave much as consumers of any other product or service do. They tend to think of the familiar and the well-known before the less familiar and the obscure. They operate with a set of restrictions (budgetary, aesthetic, etc.) which affect their choices. And - they tend to like to choose and work with their friends.

Part of successfully working with a constituency, therefore, is developing friendly relationships with these consumers.

Self-knowledge (Musically Speaking)

It stands to reason that in an overcrowded field the person who stands out is the one who has something very special - even unique - to offer. Obviously, you are in the best position to know what you have that is unique. For many artists, defining and articulating what these special qualities are, specifically rather than generally, is very difficult. But it is absolutely essential.

• If you don't know what about you is special, those who don't know you certainly won't know;

• If you don't know, you won't be able to tell anyone;

• If you can't tell anyone, then you may not get the opportunity to show what you have to offer to an audience, and they won't get to hear these special qualities for themselves.

Specifics

Once the principle is accepted that it is not enough to be good, but that you must let others know that you're good, you can follow some quite specific guidelines in moving toward making a consistent and fulfilling life in music. It is useful to keep in mind that starting out in music requires the same investment of time, money and marketing creativity as starting a small business. It also may require the same kind of hard-nosed business decisions; how scarce hours are best spent, how resources -financial and otherwise - can be put to maximum use.

To stick with the analogy, like any business person the musician needs:

• Credentials

• Effective communications materials

• A supportive network of customers

• The ability to deliver the goods when the job has been landed.

The first sections of this book will deal with both amassing performance and other credentials and assembling the physical materials with which an artist represents him or herself to the world.

II. Written and Visual Materials

We live in a visual culture, where much of the time what you see is what you believe. No matter how good your CD is it may not get played unless your supporting materials, both written and pictorial, are intriguing enough to convince someone to listen to it. These materials have to look professional. In our advertising-infused society, your potential customers, whatever their musical background, are almost certainly very visually sophisticated; less than professional looking materials imply less than professional quality artists. Your materials must be attractive and must convey an arresting, accurate message about you.

On the positive side, with the almost universal availability of computers and laser printers, some of the materials you will need can be produced very cheaply and can be very slick. On the negative side, some materials - notably photos - are expensive, and all require regular updating.

The most basic materials that a musician needs are a biography and a picture. In addition to these, at some point you may want to put together a complete press kit, which would contain reproductions of reviews and other supporting materials and perhaps a flyer, as well as the preceding materials. If you are presenting a concert, you will need some kind of advertising piece (a flyer, postcard, or brochure) which will let the public know about the event. We will discuss each of these in order. The materials which composers use to introduce themselves and their work to the world are specialized, and will be discussed in the chapter specifically directed to them; nonetheless, composers should read the following materials, and note the general principles which apply to everyone. Items such as press releases and pitch letters, which are sent to the press together with these materials, will be discussed in Chapter VII.

While reading this section, keep in mind that its aim is not to teach you the technical details of photography, flyer design, proofreading language, printing terms, etc., though you may want to learn something about these from one of the many sources available. Rather we hope to encourage you to think as an informed and discerning consumer, and understand your specific responsibilities in the process, while keeping in mind the point of view of the recipient of your materials. For example, we will describe how to choose a photographer, what you want your pictures to look like, and how to get the resulting pictures reproduced, since that is your responsibility. We won't tell you how to take pictures, or what kind of film a photographer should use.

Biographies

What you need for a) getting performing jobs, and b) sending information on yourself to the press, managers, or others in your potential constituency, is a narrative biography. A resume - that is, a non-narrative listing of credentials and accomplishments that is often arranged in reverse chronological order - is useful for getting academic jobs, applying for arts council grants and the like, and for certain areas in the field which specifically require one (opera companies, for example, will want to see chronologically arranged resumes with lists of roles learned or performed). Should you need a resume, there are books which will tell you how to create an effective one; if you're still in school, your placement or career development office can certainly help you to put one together. However, the narrative biography is a basic tool for letting the world know what you consider to be your most important professional accomplishments and qualities.

Usually this biography will not be chronological; the fact that you began to play the snare drum at the age of two, and the names of your first teachers, will not, hopefully, be the most interesting things about you to date. Remember who's reading it: to a media person those kinds of facts probably aren't news, and a presenter, for example, is considering hiring you for the professional you are now, not for the talented child you were yesterday. (Obviously if you are extremely young, the fact that you are a prodigy may, for the time being, be most important.) The narrative biography is written much like a news story, in the inverted pyramid form; the most important information - what makes you special - is in the first paragraph, and the information becomes of lesser importance as the reader proceeds through the later paragraphs. The least important or the most general background information should end the biography.

In many cases your biography will be used as is: by presenters in their program booklets and promotional materials, by the press when writing about you or announcing your program in the paper or on the air, and by others who need to distribute information about you. There are several reasons, therefore, for using the narrative format biography:

• You're controlling both the content and the order of the information, and making sure that the things which you think are most important are those that are picked up; when you leave that decision to others, you may not be lucky in their choices.

• You're making it more likely that the press will want to put something in the paper or on the air, since you're saving them valuable time. A busy journalist won't have to extract and create a story out of a resume.

If you are advanced enough in your career to have a substantial amount of material to use for your biography, it is helpful to have several versions of different lengths available, ranging from one paragraph to a full length piece of one to three pages.

Here are examples of biographies Concert Artists Guild uses for several of our artists. All are on CAG letterhead, with our address and phone number clearly included. Your biography, in fact all of your materials, must include this kind of information.

Baritone Thomas Meglioranza has done a lot and has received considerable recognition, and it's simply a question of finding the right order to put it in. The first paragraph of this biography includes information about his winning our competition (we always put this credit up front, as the biography is a source of information about us as well as our artists) as well as the mention of his winning the 2002 Joy In Singing Award. These two awards immediately serve to legitimize our saying that he "is establishing himself as one of the most sought-after vocalists."

The second paragraph highlights the range of concert activities both coming up for Thomas as of the time of this writing, as well as important recent activities. Since Thomas is particularly interested in performing Baroque music, most of the second paragraph highlights his activities in this area of endeavor.

The third paragraph emphasizes Thomas' considerable experience performing with orchestras as well as his involvement with contemporary music. Thus, over the course of these two paragraphs, we cover our initial statement about his expertise in "a wide range of repertoire."

The last paragraph simply gives a brief recitation of his educational credits, and mentions where he resides. This information is left until last, as it is the least relevant for his booking prospects.

Note also the date at the bottom of the page: it is important for the reader to know how recently the bio has been updated and approved.

Thomas Meglioranza, baritone

Winner, 2002 Concert Artists Guild International Competition
Winner, 2002 Joy In Singing Award

Hailed for his "vocal distinction and expressive warmth" (*The Boston Globe*), American baritone Thomas Meglioranza is quickly establishing himself as one of the country's most sought after singers for a wide variety of repertoire including oratorio, opera, and orchestral works. Recently, Mr. Meglioranza was named a Winner of the Concert Artists Guild International Competition, where he was also awarded performance engagements from Rockefeller University in New York City and the Patrons for Young Artists series in Beacon, NY. He is was also named the 2002 Winner of the prestigious Joy In Singing Award.

Mr. Meglioranza's 2002-2003 engagements include recitals in New York City at Weill Recital Hall at Carnegie Hall and at Merkin Concert Hall; *Carmina Burana* and a pops concert with the Cascade Festival of Music Orchestra under Murry Sidlin; *Messiah*s with Richard Egarr and the Portland Baroque Orchestra and with the Evansville Philharmonic Orchestra under Alfred Savia; and Beethoven's *Christus am Ölberge* with Nicholas McGegan and Philharmonia Baroque. He will sing the role of Aeneas opposite soprano Evelyn Tubb for the Atlanta-based New Trinity Baroque's season opening performance and new recording of Purcell's *Dido and Aeneas*, and will appear as guest vocalist and also portray famed diarist Samuel Pepys in a special, semi-staged concert of English Restoration music with the New York Collegium in New York City. His upcoming chamber appearances include *Dover Beach* with Concertante and an appearance at New York's Cooper Union for a performance of Babbitt's *Two Sonnets*.

His 2001-2002 engagements included appearances as Apollo in Handel's *Apollo e Dafne*, and *Messiah* with the American Bach Soloists, the baritone roles in Purcell's *King Arthur* with the New York Collegium conducted by Bernard Labadie, Polyphemus in Handel's *Acis and Galatea* with the Baroque Orchestra of Iowa, the *St. John Passion* conducted by Andrew Parrott, an appearance with the Chicago Opera Theatre in the company's acclaimed production of *L'Orfeo* at the Brooklyn Academy of Music, and Monteverdi's *Vespro della B. Vergine* with the Trinity Consort.

(continued)

20

Page 2: Thomas Meglioranza, baritone   *Concert Artists Guild*

Mr. Meglioranza has made numerous appearances with orchestras in the United States, Europe, and Asia, including engagements with the Rochester Philharmonic (*Paukenmesse*), the Prague Radio Symphony (Beethoven's Mass in C), and the Thai Royal Navy Orchestra (Mozart concert arias), and he has also performed pops programs with the Charleston Symphony and the Santa Barbara Symphony. Also active in contemporary music, he will give the world premiere of a work written for him by Jorge Martin at Weill Recital Hall in the 2002-2003 season, and the Brooklyn Friends of Chamber Music recently commissioned Piere Jalbert to write a work for Mr. Meglioranza and Dutch soprano Judith van Wanroij. He has sung John Adams' *The Wound Dresser* at the Tanglewood Festival for Contemporary Music with conductor Reinbert de Leeuw, gave the Japanese premiere of Aaron Jay Kernis' song cycle *Brilliant Sky, Infinite Sky* in Sapporo (Japan) under the direction of the composer, and John Harbison's *Words from Paterson* at the Bowdoin Music Festival with Jeffrey Milarsky conducting. He has also given premiere performances of many orchestral songs written for him, including Jon Chenette's *Broken Ground* with the Des Moines Symphony, and Gavin Chuck's *Confiteor* with the Ossia Orchestra. His portrayal of Don Giovanni, under the baton of Julius Rudel with the Aspen Opera Theater, was hailed by the *Denver Post* as "a triumph." His many festival appearances include the Tanglewood, Aspen, Ravinia, Bowdoin and Pacific Music Festivals.

Mr. Meglioranza is a graduate of Grinnell College and the Eastman School of Music. He currently resides in New York City.

[September 2002]

850 Seventh Avenue Ste 1205, New York, NY 10019   Tel: 212-333-5200
Fax: 212-977-7149   CAGuild@concertartists.org   http://www.concertartists.org

By contrast, Peter Kolkay is closer to the beginning of his performing career, and does not have as many performing credits. As usual, we opened his biography with his victory at the CAG Competition. We noted his unique status as the only bassoonist to ever win our Competition, and also noted the several additional impressive performance prizes he won in addition to First Prize. Since the bassoon might be considered a "non-standard" concerto or recital instrument, we also chose to immediately mention upcoming performances to show the many facets of his already burgeoning career. We then went on in the remaining paragraphs to include his important past performances, and again included information about his additional extensive academic background.

Concert Artists Guild

Peter Kolkay, bassoon

First Prize, 2002 Concert Artists Guild International Competition
Winner, Bravo! Vail Valley Music Festival Performance Prize
Winner, Southwest Michigan Symphony Performance Prize
Winner, Brooklyn Friends of Chamber Music Performance Prize
First Prize, 2001 William C. Byrd Competition

"I have had the enormous pleasure of performing with Peter Kolkay, and I cannot praise his talents enough. He is a consummate musician, possessing both dazzling technique and exquisite musicality. What an exciting player! Anyone who might doubt the expressive power of the bassoon should hear Peter Kolkay in concert." - Ursula Oppens

The extraordinarily talented Peter Kolkay was awarded First Prize at the 2002 Concert Artists Guild International Competition, making him the first solo bassoonist ever to win First Prize at the CAG Competition in the 51 years since its inception. Mr. Kolkay was also awarded the Victor and Sono Elmaleh Award, a concerto performance with the Rochester Philharmonic Orchestra under the baton of RPO Music Director Christopher Seaman as well as chamber music performances at the Bravo! Vail Valley Music Festival, a concerto appearance with the Southwest Michigan Symphony Orchestra Prize, Robert Vodnoy, Music Director, and a recital engagement from the Brooklyn Friends of Chamber Music. Upcoming performances also include his New York recital debut at Weill Recital Hall at Carnegie Hall, and an appearance at the Savannah Onstage International Music Festival.

(continued)

850 Seventh Avenue Ste 1205, New York, NY 10019   Tel: 212-333-5200
Fax: 212-977-7149   CAGuild@concertartists.org   http://www.concertartists.org

22

Mr. Kolkay has appeared as soloist with the Flint Symphony Orchestra, the Lawrence Symphony Orchestra, the Bay View Festival Orchestra, the Musica Nova Ensemble at Eastman, and the Eastman School Symphony Orchestra. Mr. Kolkay is an avid performer of contemporary music, and has recently appeared on the American Composer's Alliance series at Christ and St. Stephen's Church in New York City, and with collaborating artists including pianist Ursula Oppens at Weill Recital Hall at Carnegie Hall in a performance of Elliott Carter's Quintet for Piano and Winds as part of special concert celebrating Mr. Carter's distinguished career. He recently recorded Mr. Carter's bassoon and viola duo *Au Quai* for Bridge Records. His competition awards include top prizes from the William C. Byrd and WAMSO Competitions. Mr. Kolkay is currently a member of the Harrisburg Symphony, and has performed with orchestras in Rochester, New Haven, and Mexico City. His performances have been broadcast on National Public Radio's Performance Today and on New York's WQXR-FM. He is also a founding member of Trio Encantar, an oboe/bassoon/piano ensemble.

In August 2002, Mr. Kolkay will assume the position of Visiting Assistant Professor of Bassoon at West Virginia University. He recently completed his doctoral studies at Yale University with Frank Morelli, and holds a master's degree from the Eastman School of Music, where he studied with John Hunt and Jean Barr. Mr. Kolkay also holds a Bachelor's degree from Lawrence University in Appleton, Wisconsin. He is a native of Naperville, Illinois.

[April 2002]

Biographies for ensembles can be difficult to write, but are easier when the group is quite experienced and active, is the Avalon String Quartet, whose bio follows. Given the extent of their activity, we start with a bold statement that includes an important critical plaudit and stakes our claim to the fact that they are a leading ensemble in this country, which the rest of the biography will then back up. The body of the biography then lists important upcoming engagements, prestigious recent engagements, and highlights of past performances. In addition, we also included a paragraph that focuses on their educational activities, as educational outreach experience is becoming more and more in demand from presenters who are becoming more deeply involved with providing their local communities with musical experiences outside of the concert hall.

24

Avalon String Quartet
Blaise Magnière, violin; Marie Wang, violin;
Che-Yen Chen, viola; Sumire Kudo, cello

First Prize, 1999 Concert Artists Guild Competition
Top Prize, 2000 ARD Munich Competition
2002-2003 Resident Quartet, The Juilliard School
2002 Chamber Music America/WQXR Record Award

Hailed as "one of the most exciting young string quartets in America" (The Washington Post), the Avalon String Quartet has established itself as one of the country's leading chamber ensembles and has earned international acclaim for the bold musicality and passionate intensity of its performances.

Highlights of the Avalon Quartet's 2002-2003 schedule include performances at Alice Tully Hall in New York City, the Library of Congress in Washington DC, the ensemble's London debut at Wigmore Hall plus a concert at the Bath International Music Festival, a tour of Canada including a return to Toronto, and concerts throughout the United States. In the summer of 2003, the Avalon Quartet will be in residence teaching at the Interlochen Center for the Arts' Advanced String Quartet Institute. Last season, the Quartet made its Mostly Mozart Festival debut at Lincoln Center, its Washington DC debut at the Library of Congress, the ensemble's Alice Tully Hall recital debut where the group gave the world premiere of a new work written for it by composer David Macbride, as well as concerts at Bargemusic, Weill Recital Hall at Carnegie Hall, the Caramoor International Music Festival, Purdue University, the Walton Arts Center, the Bravo! Vail Valley Festival, Minnesota Public Radio's St. Paul Sunday, and the ensemble's Canadian debut for the Music Toronto concert series. Summer 2002 saw the quartet performing on a three-week tour of Italy for the Emiglia Romagna Festival, and an appearance in Slovenia at the Ljubljana Festival.

The Quartet has performed throughout the United States and has given concerts for the Lively Arts Series at Stanford University, the La Jolla Chamber Music Society, Germany's ARD Kammermusikfest and Herculessaal in Munich, the Savannah Onstage International Music Festival, the Brooklyn Friends of Chamber Music, the Pittsburgh Chamber Music Society, Alice Tully Hall for the Chamber Music Society of Lincoln Center, the 92nd Street Y, the Kaye Playhouse at Hunter College, Merkin Concert Hall, Dame Myra Hess Series in Chicago, Boston's Gardner Museum Series, the Chicago Chamber Music Society, the Cleveland Museum of Art Concert Series, Ravinia Rising Stars Series, the M.I.T. Concert Series in Cambridge, MA and the Alexander Schneider Series at the New School.

(continued)

850 Seventh Avenue Ste 1205, New York, NY 10019   Tel: 212-333-5200   Fax: 212-977-7149
CAGuild@concertartists.org   http://www.concertartists.org

In the 2002-2003 season, the ensemble serves for a second year as Resident Quartet at The Juilliard School. The Avalon Quartet has been in residence at the Hartt School of Music and worked extensively with the Emerson Quartet, and previously held a similar residency with the Vermeer Quartet at Northern Illinois University. The members of the Quartet have worked with major artists including Henry Meyer, Jaime Laredo, Leon Fleischer, Peter Wiley, Gilbert Kalish, and Michael Tree, and members of the Orion, Cleveland, La Salle, Juilliard, and Tokyo string quartets. The Avalons have served as quartet in residence for the 2001 Texas Christian University/Van Cliburn Piano Institute, and in the 1999-2000 season, the ensemble served as the first Ernst Stiefel Foundation String Quartet in Residence at the Caramoor International Music Festival Center for Music and Art.

Formed in 1995 at the Norfolk Chamber Music Festival, the Quartet's numerous honors include top prize at the 2000 International Music Competition of the ARD in Germany, First Prize, the Channel Classics Prize, and the Rockport Chamber Music Festival Prize at the 1999 Concert Artists Guild Competition, and the Grand Prize at the 1998 Fischoff Chamber Music Competition.

The ensemble has also won awards the 1998 Banff International String Quartet Competition and the 1999 Melbourne International Chamber Music Competition.
In 1997, the Quartet participated in Isaac Stern's Chamber Music Workshop at Carnegie Hall. As a result, Mr. Stern invited the Avalon Quartet to perform in the Isaac Stern Chamber Music Encounters in Jerusalem and in March 2000 presented the ensemble's Carnegie Hall debut at Weill Recital Hall. The Quartet made its New York debut on the Alexander Schneider Series at the New School in 1998.

The Quartet's live performances and conversation have been featured on Chicago's WFMT-FM, New York's WQXR-FM and WNYC-FM, National Public Radio's Performance Today, Canada's CBC, Australia's ABC and France Musique. The Channel Classics label released the Avalon Quartet's debut CD, Dawn to Dusk, in February 2001 to critical acclaim. The Quartet's CD was honored with a Chamber Music America/WQXR Record Award as one of the best chamber music recordings of 2001.

[June 2002]

850 Seventh Avenue Ste 1205, New York, NY 10019   Tel: 212-333-5200   Fax: 212-977-7149
CAGuild@concertartists.org   http://www.concertartists.org

All of these biographies admittedly focus on successful performing entities, with multiple competition wins and a great deal of performance experience. If you don't have competitions or press quotes, use what you do have: your attendance at a fine music school, affiliations with particular composers or prominent musicians, specialized repertoire, or regional reputation.

In each of the biographies we have reproduced, there are one or two main points about each artist which we have tried to highlight, both through placement in the narrative and the amount of space devoted to them. In Thomas', it is a focus on experience in the world of Baroque music; in Peter's, it is the variety of engagements already offered to him; in the Avalon Quartet's, it is the highly prestigious nature of the engagements the ensemble has performed. There is no way of telling everything about an artist or ensemble in a brief biography, but the reader's interest should be piqued enough to want to know – and hear – more.

A reminder, and some advice:

DO:

Be sure that your name, address and phone number, or that of the person or organization doing your business for you, is on your biography. Putting the bio on letterhead that includes this information will do the job. It should go without saying that the biography should be neatly and attractively formatted.

AVOID:

Hyperbole, exaggeration, and praise that cannot be substantiated. The purpose of the biography is to inform in a positive way, not put something over on anyone. "One of the foremost pianists of our day" is only appropriate for someone who is, undeniably, one of the foremost pianists of our day.

Too much information. The biography probably shouldn't exceed a page or two (or three, if you're *really* famous), and it certainly shouldn't be padded to make your career to date seem more important than it is.

Photographs

We asked a friend of CAG, who once ran a performing arts series in Wisconsin, which materials were most important to her in making booking decisions. She answered that her board, which had to approve all her recommendations, was not very artistically knowledgeable, but that she could usually sell them a performer on the basis of an attractive or arresting photograph. Not a recording. We heard something similar from the very knowledgeable manager of a regional orchestra; he said that, given some good word of mouth, the right photograph would convince him that he is dealing with a serious, important artist.

A very important sales tool, your photographs should immediately tell the person seeing them something about you. They will be sent to both presenters and the press. Our specific suggestions may be ways of addressing the needs of one or the other of these groups, but can apply to all of your photos. A few general remarks, and then - a picture being worth the proverbial thousand words - some examples.

You will want to have several good photographs to use for various purposes, but the most basic one you will need is an 8" X 10" black-and-white or color glossy headshot. Headshots aren't really only heads; they are portraits which are not full figure, and can, and in the case of your formal photo *should*, include your instrument. Color is rapidly becoming the industry standard, though black-and-white is still accepted. If you are on a limited budget with your photographer, you may wish to only have yourself photographed in color, as a color photo can always be reproduced in black and white, but the reverse is obviously not possible.

Assuming now that you will have at least two photos, usually you will want one formal and one informal pose. The informal shot can include more, or all, of you, and may well be an "action" shot, perhaps showing you doing what you do. (This is always hardest for singers, since you don't want photographs with your mouth open; one journalist we've spoken with is a fan of the "perusing the score" picture in this case.) The formal picture should show you in concert dress, whether that's tux or gown, or turtlenecks and jeans - whatever characteristic clothes you wear for an evening performance. The informal shot should contrast with the formal one.

Your photo(s) must be relatively recent, and be recognizable as you, NOW. There have been far too many dismayed presenters who've waited in airport lobbies to meet artists who've already arrived, but whom they've not recognized because the only photo they've seen is a high school graduation picture. Life is full of embarrassments, but this should never be one of yours.

Your photo(s) must include your name, telephone number and address, either stripped in at the bottom or labeled on the back.

There are two reasons why artists don't regularly update their pictures. First, photo sessions are expensive. If this is your excuse you have our sympathy, but not our approval, as photos simply must be a regular part of your ongoing business expenses. Second, some artists feel that being older will keep them out of a job, and that a picture taken when they were younger will help them get a job. This is not necessarily untrue, but submitting a misleading photo simply adds one handicap to another; when the moment of reckoning arrives, you're not only old, you're unreliable and untruthful. You therefore need to find a photographer who can bring out those qualities in you which will be engaging, in one way or another, irrespective of your age.

One last comment about making sure your pictures look like you, aimed specifically at women. One of our journalist friends has frequently complained about photographers who overuse a certain look which makes all their subjects look alike: glamorous, high-cheekboned and doe-eyed. Very few of the women in the photographs actually look like that when seen in person. The reporter's feeling, and ours, is that it's great to look good, but not to look like someone else looking good. Make sure that your overall appearance and style generally correspond to the way you actually present yourself on stage.

On to the examples. The first set of pictures are of a soloist, pianist Alpin Hong. We selected these photos to demonstrate how good pictures say something very specific about an artist. In asking for reactions to Alpin Hong's performances, the words most commonly used to describe him are "engaging," "dramatic," and "charismatic." In addition, critically, Alpin has been highly praised for his sensitive interpretations of the Romantic and classical literature, but has also earned plaudits for his dramatically absorbing performances of contemporary works. To demonstrate his wide-ranging musical tastes and performance style, we chose a formal photo that in its friendly openness communicates his ability to engage an audience in his music. For his second, informal photo, we went with a contrasting pose that is highly dramatic. The qualities that set this artist apart as a musician and performer can be seen in these pictures, in his poses, clothing, even the quality of his eye contact with the camera. Similarly, managing your own career, a photograph or photographs that clearly reveal something of your performing personality can be an immeasurable asset. (Photos of Mr. Hong © 2001 Steve J. Sherman.)

ALPIN HONG, piano

concertartistsguild
850 Seventh Avenue Suite 1205
New York, NY 10019
212-333-5200

ALPIN HONG, piano

concertartistsguild
850 Seventh Avenue Suite 1205
New York, NY 10019
212-333-5200

PHOTO: STEVE J. SHERMAN

The following photos, of Antares and of violinist Michi Wiancko, illustrate another reason why you should, if possible, have both an informal and formal shot. The formal shot is one which can be used in many situations; it is serious, attractive, and shows the instrument(s). For instance, we chose the first, formal Antares photo to portray a serious, high-end chamber ensemble. The informal photo should present something different – maybe fun or unusual. One staff member described the second photo of Antares as depicting a "downtown" ensemble – hip and cutting-edge music makers.

Not every picture can, or should, demonstrate everything about a performer. (If it could, the performer would necessarily be of quite limited ability). But every picture should reveal something, and it should be the truth.

Antares

concertartistsguild

Antares

MICHI WIANCKO, VIOLIN

850 Seventh Avenue, Suite 1205
New York, NY 10019
Tel: 212-333-5200

Michi Wiancko, violin

Photos we can't show you: What not to do

The best photo examples for a book like this are probably the bad ones, those that all of us have seen which evoke snickers or wisecracks rather than smiles of admiration. Not wishing to be cruel, and being aware that the field is - all the cutthroat competition notwithstanding - a small one, we can't print them. But we can at least describe some of the obvious problems we see with some frequency, with the hope that you'll look at your own materials with a somewhat dispassionate and objective eye.

Photographs with terrible backgrounds: wrinkled backdrops, unrelated scenery, random passersby waving at the camera, etc. They're distracting and look very unprofessional.

Odd facial expressions: A photo of two young women, who would probably have described it as "cheerful," was experienced by everyone in our office as "predatory," given the predominance of teeth. Please have someone other than a loving parent look at the shots.

Problems with image: For example, come-hither may be fine, sexy can be fine, but make sure that the photo does not misrepresent the artist and/or event. Pictures that are overly sexy may be misleading (unless your performances do, in fact, offer something considerably off the beaten path for a classical musician). This principle is obviously true for any other striking, but possibly inappropriate, image.

How-To

Finding a photographer isn't hard, but finding a good one, and the right one, can be. The local photography studio that does weddings and bar mitzvahs is usually not the right place to go; they have little or no experience with the needs, both professional and technical, of the classical music field. The best way to find the right photographer, as with everything else, is to do some research and look at other musicians' photos. After a while you should begin to see which photographer's work you like, and what kind of pictures might work for you. Since this is an expensive investment and a very important one, consider the decision carefully.

Budget suggestions

- If you are still in school, and have access to photography students who are in the process of building up their own portfolios, you may have an ideal opportunity to get some wonderful pictures for very little or no money. You might need to provide the photographer with somewhat more direction and guidance than you would a seasoned professional who has often worked with performers, but the student may well give you more time, effort, and care than her more experienced colleague can.

- Photographers who work regularly with actors or other entertainers rather than with classical musicians may charge less. This may be a very good option, particularly for singers. Again, you may have to provide guidance and be aware that your requirements may be somewhat different from those of the subjects they usually work with, but you also may get a fresh point of view and some very interesting pictures as a result.

- If you live or come from anywhere other than New York, remember that New York City prices are generally higher for professional services, photography included. Even if you are professionally based in New York City, you might explore getting your pictures taken elsewhere, if you can find the right photographer familiar with the needs of musicians.

When you do schedule a photo session, discuss its length and requirements with the photographer in advance, and know what you're getting into. Be prepared to spend at least several hours. Bring several changes of clothing for both formal and informal shots as described above. Make sure that if you play the piano there will be one in the studio, or arrange for a location that will have one. Know what the location offers in the way of background if you're not working in the photographer's studio. Bring your instrument and any other materials that you may require.

The photographer will make a contact sheet of the session, from which you will usually select two photos that you like. Depending on your agreement, the photographer will make "portraits" from each selected shot, which are slightly retouched, good quality 8X10's; these are what you're buying. These portraits will be your visual equivalent of a master tape. ***You'll duplicate them, but never send these originals to anyone.*** The negatives are the property of the photographer, and you will never own them. The artistic content of the portraits is also the property of the photographer; you must credit him whenever the photo is used. (He needs to get work too, and this is how he gets his name around.)

Since a good photographer is very busy, and since she doesn't want to spend all her time making duplicates of photos for your press purposes (and since it would be far too expensive for you if reproduced on that basis), she will usually give you permission to have the portrait commercially duplicated in quantity. This is the standard arrangement. The arrangement may vary with different photographers, or in the case of color sessions which result in slides, so be very careful to get everything clear before beginning.

Take your portraits to a commercial photo duplication shop that specializes in bulk orders and have them make a copy negative from each one, which you will then use whenever you need prints. The copy negative is an 8X10 negative which the duplication house may be willing to keep on file for you. Order glossy prints to be made from the copy negative in a quantity that will be both useful and economical. (Don't go to a FotoMat type of place, as they will be far too expensive for this kind of work.) Get them to strip in your name and contact information if at all possible (see the photo examples above). This will save having to type or print labels and affix them to the back of each picture, and it doesn't cost much extra.

Remember, every photo you send out, like everything else you send out, must have your name and at least a phone number on it. Some variation of Murphy's Law surely says that if something can get lost or separated, it will. The best picture in the world won't help you if no one knows who it is.

A very important rule: Don't send a picture, or any other expensive piece of material, unless you are reasonably sure that it will get looked at or read, and that the recipient won't immediately throw it away.

Pictures and other materials will almost never be returned, even if you've provided a stamped, self-addressed envelope. It's too expensive for you to send materials, and too annoying for the recipient to get them, when they haven't been requested and aren't needed.

The Press Kit

When involved in more extensive sales, or when more elaborate publicity is required, you will probably want to put together a press kit. The term "press kit" is somewhat misleading, since it is used for sales and management as well as press purposes. The press kit is simply a compilation of your materials, put together in a convenient way and immediately identifiable as yours. Physically it is a folder, which can be an inexpensive pocket folder from the stationery store, which will contain your biography, pictures, and additional supporting materials. Since the additional materials will be there to support the story set out in the biography, they will be those items which amplify your basic sales points: i.e., feature articles and reviews (which prove that you've played many different places and the critics love you); a flyer (which demonstrates that you are a savvy performer who can help them with their publicity materials); a repertoire list (showing that you have an extensive and interesting repertoire).

The following example shows some of the contents of Alpin Hong's press kit, including his flyer, his biography, one review, and one feature article. In the actual kit there are many of each of these last two items. The folder itself has a copy of the flyer pasted to it. We don't include photos, since the flyer is essentially pictures with the addition of text.

ALPIN HONG
piano

WINNER

2001 Concert Artists Guild
International Competition

"...A pianistic firebrand...clear and persuasive...his thunderous reading
was remarkable for its nearly orchestral breadth and coloration." — *New York Times*

"It was a tour de force in the original, absolute sense. Hong evoked a kind of Beatlemania
when he came on stage, and the crowd made so much clamor after he finished..." — *Santa Barbara News-Press*

concertartistsguild

BOOKING INFORMATION
Brian Bumby, Senior Vice President

Concert Artists Guild
850 Seventh Avenue, Suite 1205   P: 212.333.5200
New York, NY 10019   F: 212.977.7149

ALPIN HONG piano

"A pianistic firebrand…he kept the voltage consistently high," reads a recent *New York Times* review of Alpin Hong's New York recital debut. Equally captivating in his interpretations of Schubert, Shostakovich or Schoenberg, Alpin Hong thrills audiences with his stunning virtuosity, artistic vision and irreverent style. First Prize Winner at the 2001 Concert Artists Guild International Competition, his charismatic performance won him standing ovations and the jury's unanimous vote. The first pianist in eight years to win CAG's highest honor, Mr. Hong was the recipient of four additional performance prizes including his New York debut at Weill Recital Hall at Carnegie Hall, solo appearances with the Indian Hill Symphony, Orchestra X and at Market Square Concerts. Recent and upcoming performance highlights include the Music Academy of the West, Bowdoin Summer Music Festival, the Frick

Art & Historical Center in Pittsburgh, Kansas City Friends of Chamber Music, Sinfonietta Cracovia in Krakow, Hoam Arts Center in Seoul, Asociacion Nacional de Conciertos in Panama, as well as performances with the Greeley Philharmonic and Wartburg Symphony.

Mr. Hong's recent Carnegie Hall debut garnered tremendous praise from *New York Times* critic Allan Kozinn, who cited his performance for its "crystalline energy," "clear and persuasive ideas" and "nearly orchestral breadth and coloration." A Juilliard graduate who studied with Jerome Lowenthal, Alpin Hong performed his orchestral debut with the Kalamazoo Symphony at age 10. He has since developed an international career, recently performing with the Korean Broadcast Symphony (KBS), at the Dorothy Chandler Pavilion in Los Angeles and at New York's Alice Tully and Avery Fisher Halls. Remarkable renditions of the Stravinsky *Firebird Suite* at

the Music Academy of the West won him a series of passionate reviews in the *Santa Barbara News-Press:* "A demonic flourish named Alpin Hong…evoked a kind of Beatlemania when he came on stage. The notes fell crashing to the stage like cluster bombs with perfect pitch; the interludes, eyes of the storm, came stately or exquisitely tender."

As a teenage virtuoso, Alpin Hong won the 1994 Los Angeles Spotlight Awards Competition, 1993 SYMF Competition and 1989 Stravinsky Piano Competition. He was invited to participate in the inaugural 1990 Soviet-American Piano Institute in Moscow and performed at master classes with Andre Watts, Emanuel Ax and Daniel Pollack. Alpin Hong currently resides in New York City.

" Alpin Hong went over the top, down the other side and all the way over the top again!" - *New York Times*

"I can't imagine a more sensitive, profound interpretation of Liszt's *Benediction of God in Solitude* than the one Hong played Sunday afternoon. There were clouds of shimmering sound and achingly tender melodies. Having prefaced his performance by reading the poem on which the piece is based, Hong intensified the experience of a renewal of religious faith." -*The Harrisburg Patriot-News*

ALPIN HONG, piano
First Prize, 2001 Concert Artists Guild Competition

"Alpin Hong went over the top, down the other side, and all the way over the top again!" reads a recent *New York Times* review of the young pianist's daring performance of Aaron Jay Kernis' *Superstar Etude.* Equally captivating in his interpretations of Schubert, Shostakovich or Schoenberg, Alpin Hong thrills audiences with his stunning virtuosity, artistic vision, and irreverent style. First Prize Winner at the 2001 Concert Artists Guild International Competition, his charismatic performance won him standing ovations and the jury's unanimous vote. The first pianist in eight years to win CAG's highest honor, Mr. Hong was the recipient of four additional performance prizes including his New York debut at Weill Recital Hall at Carnegie Hall, solo appearances with the Indian Hill Symphony, Orchestra X and at Market Square Concerts. Recent and upcoming performance highlights include the Sinfonietta Cracovia, New York's Rockhotel Pianofest and Rockefeller University, Seoul's Hoam Arts Center, the Frick Arts Centre in Pittsburgh, Kansas City Friends of Chamber Music, the Chamber Music Society of Little Rock, the Merkin Concert Hall 50th Anniversary Celebration, Maverick Concerts, the Asociacion Nacional de Conciertos in Panama, as well as concerto performances with the Greeley Philharmonic and Wartburg Symphony.

Mr. Hong's recent Carnegie Hall debut garnered tremendous praise from *New York Times* critic Allan Kozinn, who cited his performance for its "crystalline energy," "clear and persuasive ideas" and "remarkable breadth and coloration." A Juilliard graduate who studied with Jerome Lowenthal, Alpin Hong performed his orchestral debut with the Kalamazoo Symphony at age 10. He has since given numerous concerts, recently performing with the Korean Broadcast Symphony (KBS), at the Dorothy Chandler Pavilion in Los Angeles, and at New York's Alice Tully and Avery Fisher Halls. A remarkable rendition of Luciano Berio's *Points on the Curve to Find* at the 2001 Focus! Festival in New York won him another *New York Times* mention: "It's like some crazed piano concerto, and Alpin Hong excitingly dispatched the fiendish solo part, replete with oscillating tremolos that made his arms a blur."

As a teenage virtuoso, Alpin Hong won the 1994 Los Angeles Spotlight Awards Competition, 1993 SYMF Competition and 1989 Stravinsky Piano Competition. He was invited to participate in the inaugural 1990 Soviet-American Piano Institute in Moscow, performed at master classes with Andre Watts, Emanuel Ax and Daniel Pollack, and participated at the Music Academy of the West, Aspen and Bowdoin Summer Music Festivals. Alpin Hong currently resides in New York City.

Concert Artists Guild 850 Seventh Avenue, New York, NY 10019 • Tel.: (212) 333-5200
Fax: (212) 977-7149 • E-mail: Sshaiman@concertartists.org • Internet: www.concertartists.org

The New York Times

ON THE WEB

October 16, 2001

Crystalline energy from a firebrand

By Allan Kozinn

During his years as a Juilliard student, Alpin Hong performed in several of the school's contemporary-music concerts and left the impression that he is a pianistic firebrand, unfazed by the difficulties of new music. His performance on Thursday evening — part of his prize as the first-prize winner of the Concert Artist Guild Competition last spring — showed that Mr. Hong is not much more restrained in the standard repertory.

That is not a complaint. In a program that included works by Clementi, Brahms, Liszt, Ravel, Stravinsky and Shostakovich, Mr. Hong kept the voltage consistently high, but energy was not all he had to offer. His ideas about the works at hand were clear and persuasive, and as hard driven as his readings were, it was clear that he kept stylistic distinctions firmly in mind.

In Shostakovich's Prelude and Fugue No. 15, for example, the counterpoint remained crisp and sharp- edged, no matter how dense the textures became. In Clementi's Sonata in F minor (Op. 13, No. 6), by contrast, the tensions between Classicism and nascent Romanticism in the work came to life in the form of an elegantly crystalline top line and a heavy, muscular bass. Mr. Hong's

account of Ravel's "Valses Nobles et Sentimentales" touched on the full spectrum of Ravel's ballroom portrait, from the powerful and sharply accented to the more gently perfumed. And his thunderous reading of three sections from Stravinsky's "Firebird" was remarkable for its nearly orchestral breadth and coloration.

Also on the program were two Liszt works — the Concert Étude No. 3 and "Bénédiction de Dieu dans la Solitude" — and Brahms's "Paganini" Variations, Book II. There were moments in the Brahms when virtuosity edged into harshness, but never for long. And Lizst's "Bénédiction" was at its most poetic.

One might expect that the exertions inherent in this program might have left Mr. Hong drained. But there were encores as well, the last of which was a wholly uninhibited performance of Aaron Jay Kernis's "Superstar Étude No. 1," complete with feet and elbows on the keyboard, and bluesy vocalizations in the final bars.

Concert Artists Guild 850 Seventh Avenue, New York, NY 10019 ▪ Tel.: (212) 333-5200
Fax: (212) 977-7149 ▪Elan Gore, Vice-President ▪ E-mail: elan@concertartists.org ▪ www.concertartists.org

Korea Herald
April 6, 2002

Virtuoso surmounts tragedy through music

His body sways, his face cringes and his fingers emote the sorrow of the legato notes. Pianist Alpin Hong's mastery is evident in his technique but also in the intensity of his playing.

Having endured tragedy as a young child, Hong found solace in his music, and in the process, discovered a fiery talent that has recently gained him international recognition. At the age of 25, this Korean-American virtuoso has come to Korea to showcase his classical and expressive performance.

When Hong was 12 years old, his parents died in a car accident. In an interview with The Korea Herald, he recalled the comforting role that music has played in his life since. "It's been my best friend. It was the one thing I could always fall back on, as an emotional support," he said.

Last year, Hong won first place at the Concert Artists Guild International Competition in New York, an accomplishment that has paved the way for his rising musical fame. As the winner, Hong was given a three-year management contract, a recording contract and the opportunity to perform with renowned symphonies, including a debut at Carnegie Hall.

He is currently touring internationally and performing in Poland and China in addition to Korea. His dynamic performances have already won plaudits from reviewers at the New York Times and several esteemed music publications.

"I had never thought I could make a career out of this. It's not every job where

after you come home from work, everyone stands up and claps for you," he said.

Considering his success, it is hard to believe Hong's career was on another track just three years ago. After his parents died, Hong was determined to support himself and his brother, and knew a career in music had no financial guarantees. So he chose medicine like his father.

"My father had given us everything we had ever wanted or needed. I kind of vowed to myself I would follow that," he said.

In his last year of premedical studies at UCLA, however, Hong was invited to perform in Korea. A Korean government official had seen him perform in Los Angeles and had selected him to play in a concert with the Korean Broadcast Symphony (KBS). The opportunity came at a crucial moment, Hong said, a point at which he had to decide once and for all which career path he would take.

"I was prepared to give up performance forever to be a doctor," he said.

The performance in Seoul revived his musical passion, and he returned to the United States with a resolve to take the dive into a career in music, which promised risks but possibly great rewards as well.

"(The concert) showed me I still had the capability to do it, and it showed me how much it still thrills me. I really couldn't face giving it up."

Concert Artists Guild 850 Seventh Avenue, New York, NY 10019 ▪ Tel.: (212) 333-5200
Fax: (212) 977-7149 ▪ E-mail: brian@concertartists.org ▪ www.concertartists.org

Hong's childhood was a mix of Korean and American, not uncommon among second-generation Korean-Americans. Raised in Battlecreek, Mich., he skateboarded with his friends but also followed a grueling schedule of afterschool lessons, including piano, violin and jazz clarinet.

"(Korean-American) parents see it as a necessity that their kids do some kind of music or dance, something artistic," he said.

Hong remembers that at the piano recitals he played in, nearly half of the participants were also of Korean decent.

"It's a desire for excellence, I think, a need to show the world or show America that Korean people have this special quality about them," he said.

Hong admits that like many other children he hated practicing but now appreciates the gift that his parents have given him.

"Music's the one thing that I've had that has continued from that beautiful time, Edenic existence I had."

Now a rising star, Hong's playing style has developed a visual distinctiveness as well as a technical one. Audiences have noted his dramatic facial expressions, saying he almost appears to be laughing or crying on stage.

"I don't do it consciously. I think it's because my music for me is a pure outlet of my emotions, whether it is love, fear or sadness."

Hong does not shy away from the performance aspect of his art either. In his last competition piece at the Concert Artists Guild International Competition, Hong played Aaron Jay Kernis' "Superstar" Etude No. 1, in which he played chords with his feet and wailed Elvis-style.

"The piece gets harder and harder until you have to use your feet, and in the end, you're finally singing because there's nothing left you can do," Hong explained, smiling. The unconventional program won him a unanimous vote from the judges, a feat last achieved eight years ago. Critics have since described his idiosyncratic playing as "fiendish" and have bestowed upon him the sobriquet of "firebrand."

To Hong, however, his musicality is more a testament to his renewed faith after a darker time.

"The fact that I'm here, playing this piece, gives me a chance to show people that life is beautiful, no matter how hard it gets."

Reviews and other inserts

A review can be reproduced in its entirety if it's all positive. You can clip the article, the name of the publication (the masthead) and the date out of the paper, and neatly and carefully glue them to a piece of paper which has your name, address and contact information on it. Have the sheet photocopied, and put it in the kit. (If the only copy you can get of the review is in very bad shape and won't reproduce cleanly, it is permissible to re-type it, as long as you don't change anything.) Alternatively, you can print the article directly off the Internet. You can, of course, leave out the last line, or paragraph, if that's where the critic decided to put the negative comments. If there are less than ideal comments throughout the body of the review, or even only one good comment in a largely negative review, it's obviously better to use only excerpts.

If you have a feature article which is not a review - but is flattering - by all means use it in your press kit.

In excerpts, as in all reproduced written materials, make sure that all the quotes are properly ascribed. You can combine a group of review excerpts onto one clearly identified sheet of paper. Make sure the stationery you use is, as always, identified as yours, and includes information on how to reach you.

Beware of having too many dots, showing where you've left words or phrases out, since your quote will lose credibility (in other words, no "Mr. Jones was very ... good"). Be careful when quoting excerpts from reviews to let common sense guide your choices; you're not trying to put anything over on anyone, but rather letting the world know that something positive has been written about you. As long as you're not misrepresenting the intentions of your critics, and they actually did have something good to say, you're probably excerpting responsibly.

50

ANTARES

Vesselin Gellev, violin
Rebecca Patterson, violoncello
Garrick Zoeter, clarinet
Eric Huebner, piano

PRESS EXCERPTS

"Concert Artists Guild has been lucky with new-music ensembles lately. A few years ago the superb *eighth blackbird* won it's annual competition, and on Tuesday evening its season at Weill Recital Hall opened with Antares, a high-energy quartet from Connecticut that won first prize last year…. The players made a vivid impression…. The performance included some especially winning solo turns…."

The New York Times

"A wonderful resounding and expansive expressiveness … a Brahmsian array of sounds and emotions…."

The Los Angeles Times

"Powerful virtuosity and striking razor-sharp ensemble playing…. Their stellar technique, enthusiasm, and commitment carried the day."

The Chicago Tribune

"… consistently excellent…."

The Strad

"The [ensemble] played with striking energy and panache."

The Detroit Free Press

850 Seventh Avenue Ste 1205, New York, NY 10019   Tel: 212-333-5200 Fax: 212-977-7149
CAGuild@concertartists.org   http://www.concertartists.org

A repertoire sheet will be useful if you're sending the kit to a presenter. You also might use a repertoire sheet to send to a conductor or orchestra manager.

Concert Artists Guild

ANTARES
Repertoire

-- QUARTETS --

Adler, Samuel	Aeolus: God of the Winds (1978)	18'
Etezady, Roshanne	Mother of Pearl (1998)	8'
Freund, Stefan	Dodecaphunphrolic (1997)	4'
Hindemith, Paul	Quartet (1938)	24'
Kirchner, Volker David	Exil (1994)	20'
Laderman, Ezra	Scenes From and Imagines Life (1998)	18'
Laderman, Ezra	Remembering and Unremembered Life (1999)	15'
Lerdahl, Fred	Marches (1992)	15'
Loevendie, Theo	Cycles (1992)	15'
Mackey, John	Dementia (2000)	9'
Messiaen, Olivier	Quatuor pour la fin du temps	55'
Muskal, Tamar	Harold and the Purple Crayon (1997)	20'
Newman, Maria	Terpsichorie, dance variations	18'
Putz, Kevin	Simaku (1996)	7'
Rabl, Walter	Quartet (1896)	22'
Schickele, Peter	Quartet (1986)	16'
Schiff, David	Divertimento from Gimpel the Fool (1985)	18'
Schneller, Oliver	Tapoi (2000)	8'
Schumann, Robert	Quartet in E-flat, Op. 47 (1842) (arr.)	25'
Stravinsky, Igor	L'histoire du Soldat (1915) (arr.)	15'
Takemitsu, Toru	Quatrain II (1987)	15'
Tsontakis, George	Eclipse (1995)	20'

--TRIOS--

Bartók, Béla	Contrasts (1938)	(vn, cl, pn)	16'
Beethoven, Ludwig van	Trio, Op, 11 (1798)	(cl, vc, pn)	20'
Beethoven, Ludwig van	Piano Trio in c, Op. 1, No. 3		25'
Brahms, Johannes	Trio in a, Op, 114 (1886)	(cl, vc, pn)	28'
Carter, Elliott	Con Leggerezza Pensos (1990)	(vn, cl, vc)	5'
Dahl, Ingolf	Concerto a Tré (1957)	(vl, cl, vc)	22'
Ives, Charles	Largo (1901)	(vn, cl, pn)	10'
Milhaud, Darius	Suite	(vn, cl, pn)	13'
Mozart, W.A.	Trio, K. 498 (1786)	(vc, cl, pn)	18'
Rorem, Ned	End of Summer	(vn, cl, pn)	15'
Shostakovich, Dmitri	Piano Trio, Op 67	(vn, vc, pn)	25'

850 Seventh Avenue Ste 1205, New York, NY 10019   Tel: 212-333-5200 Fax: 212-977-7149
CAGuild@concertartists.org   http://www.concertartists.org

Flyers

Flyers can be used for a variety of purposes. A flyer can provide much of the information discussed above in a single sheet for general use. If your design allows for some blank space, it can be surprinted with specific information about a particular performance and serve as a concert flyer. These days, we often print two versions of flyers, one longer with space at the bottom for this purpose. On the front of our artists' flyers, we include the following, in order of importance:

- Name and instrument or voice type. (An ensemble may choose not to list names of individuals and their instruments on the front.)

- A photograph, usually a formal shot

- A quote from a newspaper review (if you have one), or other short and intriguing verbiage

- Representation information (management, record label, etc).

The following example is the front of the flyer for the ensemble Antares.

concertartistsguild

ANTARES

First Prize
2002 Concert Artists Guild
International Competition
Winner
Victor and Sono Elmaleh Award

"Powerful virtuosity and striking razor-sharp ensemble playing."
– *The Chicago Tribune*

"A wonderful resounding and expansive expressiveness –
a Brahmsian array of sounds and emotions." – *The Los Angeles Times*

On the back:

        • Another photograph, usually the informal shot;

        • More quotes (if you've got them) and credits;

        • A brief biography;

        • Recording and other credits;

        • Booking address, phone number and contact person.

Example: Flyer back

This format is variable, but the flyer should be concise, feature a good picture or pictures, include some interesting short written information, and perhaps have some blank space available where you or a presenter could surprint the specifics about an event.

concertartistsguild

Booking Information:

Brian D. Bumby
Senior Vice President

P: 212.333.5200
F: 212.977.7149

Concert Artists Guild
850 Seventh Avenue
Suite 1205
New York, NY 10019

Brian@concertartists.org
www.concertartists.org

ANTARES

Vesselin Gellev
violin

Rebecca Patterson
cello

Garrick Zoeter
clarinet

Eric Huebner
piano

The extraordinary chamber ensemble Antares was named First Prize Winner of the 2002 Concert Artists Guild Competition and also received the Victor and Sono Elmaleh Award, the WQXR Prize and numerous performance engagements. Antares draws from a vast and colorful repertoire for the piano-clarinet quartet formation as well as its various trio permutations. Its programs span the traditional eras of classical music from the 18th, 19th, and 20th centuries to performances of new works created for the ensemble. Formerly known as the Elm City Ensemble, Antares has won top prizes in four national chamber music competitions as well as a 1999 CMA/ASCAP Award for Adventurous Programming.

Highlights of Antares' performance schedule include the ensemble's New York debut at Weill Recital Hall at Carnegie Hall, the La Jolla Chamber Music Society, the Hancher Auditorium at the University of Iowa, the Krannert Center at the University of Illinois, Market Square Concerts, the Chautauqua Institution, the Friends of Music at Queens College in Charlotte, NC and the Brooklyn Friends of Chamber Music, where Antares gives the world premiere of a new work by the award-winning composer Derek Bermel. Notable past performances include the Kennedy Center in Washington DC, the New Victory Theater in New York City, a three-part series at the Festival of Arts and Ideas New Haven, CT, the quartet's Canadian debut in London, Ontario and a collaboration with the Parsons Dance Company at the Joyce Theatre in New York City.

Actively involved in commissioning new music, Antares has worked with comoposers including Ezra Laderman, Stephan Freund, Kevin Puts and members of the Minimum Security Composers Collective. The ensemble's two most recent commissions are by John Mackey, as part of the ensemble's collaboration with the Parsons Dance Company, and by Oliver Schneller through a Meet the Composer grant. Antares recorded Ned Rorem's *Summer Trio* on the Newport Classic label and has also recorded works by Ezra Laderman and David Schiff.

Antares is currently the ensemble in residence at Wesleyan University, has also been in residence at Columbia University for two years and has served as ensemble in residence at the Festival Eleazar de Carvalho in Brazil. Antares is a member of the Connecticut State Commission on the Arts Touring Roster, which provides partial funding for various programs throughout Connecticut and New England. Under its auspices, the ensemble performs concerts, lecture/performances, master classes and school outreach programs.

Photos: Steve J. Sherman

"Striking energy and panache." *– The Detroit Free Press*

"Consistently excellent." *– The Strad*

Costs

Very roughly, the cost of producing a four-color flyer might run as follows:

Photography $1500

Design $400

Printing (2500) $1200

Total: $3100

You may already have photographs; you may be able to do your own typesetting on a laser printer; and perhaps you know a designer who will donate his services. In this case, you're left only with the printing cost, which is quite enough. Shop around outside of New York for printing, even if you're based here; often you can get a real bargain and not lose quality. The printing cost listed above is based on using coated (that is, shiny) stock.

Flyers can be as plain or as elaborate as you want or can afford. In general, you can save money by using one color (which may be black) and white; additional colors cost, and full-color is most expensive, though it is widely used these days. Your choice of paper will also affect the cost, as will the number of photos, since reproducing pictures is more expensive than reproducing text.

Aesthetics are important, and a good looking flyer can be very helpful; however, tastes differ, and ours may not be yours. What you need to do is to look around and see what you like. If you can find a designer whose work you very much admire, and who's affordable, by all means hire her. As we mentioned in the "budget" section in regard to photos, if you're in school, and can hook up with a gifted design student who is building up a portfolio, you might get something very striking for little or no money. Similarly, if you are working with a non-profit group, you might be able to get professional design services donated. If you know a good professional designer, ask.

One additional use for a flyer: it can be pasted to the front of the press kit folder to personalize it. This is very commonly done, and can look very good. If you're having flyers printed in large quantities, it might be useful to ask that several hundred be printed only on one side (the front) for this purpose.

Probably, wonderful flyers have gotten people jobs; probably, ordinary flyers haven't lost anyone a job. Terrible flyers could though. As with all your materials, the flyer must reflect something about you, and must never give anyone a reason to believe that you are anything other than completely professional.

Concert Flyers

Concert flyers come in various forms, from very simple postcards to actual flyers to elaborate season brochures. Budget and scale will guide your choice. You can use a general flyer, if you have one, surprinted or stickered with the specific concert information, or you can design a flyer specifically for the event.

For a single concert, make sure that your flyer (or postcard, or whatever you've chosen) contains the standard minimum information of the news story, i.e., who, what, when and where. Why isn't necessary, though a newspaper quote or some other teaser may tell the reader why they might want to attend. In addition you need to include the following:

• Ticket price(s), including applicable discounts if any

• Repertoire information

• Assisting artists

When putting these together, remember that you will be:

• Sending them direct mail;

• Handing them out, or stuffing them into programs of prior events at the same venue;

• Posting them in strategic places, to make sure that someone comes.

Your design should accommodate as many of these possible uses as you will need. That is, if you're mailing the flyers, make sure they have space on one side for an address label and a return address. If you're posting them, make sure that everything reads coherently (not upside down) when unfolded.

Budget Flyers: When you're just getting started, and want to publicize an event

We made a flyer a number of years ago for the debut performance of a wind quintet which had never played together before; they still had no picture, no newspaper quote and no group credentials. They also had almost no money, and had to do the flyer cheaply. The flyer was formatted on someone's laser printer, and printed on one side of the paper in red on white glossy stock. We placed a large circle with the name of the group - "Solar Winds" - in the center of the flyer, listed the players underneath, and put the information about the event at the bottom. The piece looked fine but a bit bare, but yellow magic marker added by hand around the red circle (looking like a sun?) made it that much more cheerful. The brief written material below the artists' names described their individual credentials, since they didn't have ensemble credentials as yet. The same flyer could have been used for other performances as well, or - if desperate - for general booking, with contact rather than performance information at the bottom of the piece. A similar piece could probably be printed for about $150 now, for 1000 copies.

Concert Flyers
Embarrassing errors checklist

All of the following are errors that we have made at one time or another, and we hope to help you avoid them. **When proofing your flyers, look for:**

Date	Make sure that the day, month, year (believe it or not, we've screwed that one up once), and exact hour of the concert are all correct.
Address	Since Concert Artists Guild, for example, has an address different from that of the hall where our concerts are performed, we have to include both our return address and that of the hall. In addition, make sure that you have included the phone number of the hall box office, again being particularly careful if the number is different from the one you would usually list for contact information.
Spelling	Check spelling of performers' names, including all assisting artists. Do remember to list all the assisting artists; one of our most embarrassing moments was when we failed to list the pianist for a violin recital. The pianist is both marvelous and a great friend of ours, and we - and he - were devastated.
Layout orientation	When the printer gives you the "blue" - the blueprint proof copy of the piece - to check for smudges or errors, make sure that nothing will come out upside down when the flyer's folded, and that the front/back orientation of the postcard is correct.

III. Making a Recording

*The following chapter and the next about the Internet, have been written by
Oliver Brewer, a young musician with a special interest and expertise in these areas.*

There are many reasons why one might want to make a recording.
Making a recording compels you, the performer, to closely examine an
interpretation/conception of the score; it allows you to study your own
performance; and it requires you to perform at the highest level possible. You
will most likely use an edited recording to send to presenters, managers,
competitions, record companies, potential employers, and schools, and ultimately
you might want to make a recording to have material for a distributable compact
disc.

Next comes the question, "What do I put on my recording?" Certainly it
depends on the purpose of the recording. For all recordings that you make,
however, you will want the end product of your recording to be the highest level
of playing attainable. Beyond that, your recording should be something that
reflects your unique musical character and strengths, made possible with high-
quality audio and engineering.

Sources of Material

Determining what purpose your CD or tape will serve is most important.
Your recording, whether a competition entry or CD to sell at your concerts,
permanently imprints your musicianship – good or bad. Assembling the
materials and setting up the process of creating a CD of your music making will
require strategic planning.

Professional Recordings. A professional recording by an engineer will be the
"best foot forward" approach. This type of recording will most likely have the
highest quality audio and will sound comparable to the highly polished CDs
released on major record labels to which listeners have become accustomed – and
indeed now expect.

Concert performances, including your school recitals. Remember to edit out, or
have the engineer edit out, all but a very little of the applause. The first burst of
enthusiasm, and a fade-out after about 2-3 seconds, should let your listener know

that your performance was appreciated, without belaboring the point. In using live performance materials you're trading off recording quality for the special feel of the live performance; but be careful that the trade off is worthwhile, i.e., that you still can be effectively heard. If the recording was made by your uncle, holding his Brand X tape machine on his lap next to candy unwrapping and coughing neighbors, the person listening to the recording may not be able to fully appreciate just how terrific the performance was.

Radio broadcasts. If you perform on the radio, certainly ask if you can get a copy of the tape, since it will almost always be of very high quality. Radio stations are usually very nice about this, though you may have to pay a small charge for the actual tape.

Tapes made with high-quality portable equipment. You can probably use these when you're starting out, if you're careful to use the best equipment possible, control ambient noise, edit out extraneous material, and listen carefully to make sure that the quality of the performance comes through. It goes without saying that the performances should be especially good, since you won't be able to have the gloss of professional sound nor the excitement of the concert hall.

Labeling

Writing with a sharpie marker on the front of your CD is probably not the best idea. Your recorded materials should be packaged and labeled carefully and clearly. Quite inexpensively, you can purchase labels to be fed through your home computer's printer. Always assume that anything you give anyone will be misplaced, or at least separated from your other materials. At the very least your recording should include your name (unless you're specifically told by a competition or audition committee not to do so), the works being performed, and other relevant program information.

A Word about Video

Video may supplement your recorded materials, but for most solo and traditional chamber ensembles, there may not be any significant value in producing a professional video for sales purposes. Video can, however, convey the drama of a performance that may not be communicated via audio alone (e.g., special lighting, dance, or performances that are explicitly visual). Performers that have a uniquely theatrical element, such as a percussion quartet, will benefit from a video recording.

More importantly, however, it is worth noting the pedagogical value in watching a recorded performance or lesson. A video recording can reveal aspects of your performance that you're often unable to accurately review based on memory or recorded sound alone.

Setting up a professional recording session

Finding a Room

Paramount to a good recording is finding a good room in which to record. Classical music is recorded differently from many other types of music. Rich Mays of Sonare Recordings, a professional recording services company specializing in classical music in Savannah, Georgia, contends that with the exception of L.A., Nashville, and New York, there are few studios in the U.S. of an appropriate acoustic for someone to attempt to play classical music.

Well, what about adding in an acoustic later from a studio recording? Sonare's Rich Mays states simply that no black box will replace a great room. Although virtually all commercial recordings are "sweetened" during mastering, "we're talking about a little tweaking of the sound versus compensating for the entire room."

Finding a good room can be an involved task. Costs, availability, and location are some of the barriers to obtaining the right space to make your recording. For a good start, Mays recommends looking in your area for medium-sized empty churches with no carpet. Also, many recital halls and auditoriums are available to rent, and many of them are equipped with recording equipment.

Finding an Engineer

You must find a producer/recording engineer who has classical music experience and knowledge – someone who communicates and listens in your musical language. Rich Mays refers to this language as "phrase, timbre, pitch, and a myriad of subjective decisions summed up in the medium of communication we call music." To locate this type of engineer, ask your friends who've made recordings, other engineers in the area, or Mays suggests a good place to start: your local NPR radio station. "If your engineer can't read a score, keep looking," says Mays.

Monica Ellis of the wind quintet Imani Winds, an ensemble on the Concert Artists Guild Roster, relates the story of their first attempt to record a compact disc. One of the members of the group knew a friend with a small studio. The group showed up for their recording session and the engineer setup a microphone for each player and recorded onto multiple tracks, a common technique for recording non-classical music. Monica relates, "We discovered that there's a difference between recording classical music and pop; studio versus recording in a hall; close mic versus one mic. We work so hard [as an ensemble] on balance and dynamics," she says, and with the type of recording they did on their first CD, all of that hard work was misplaced. After taking their recording to some experts in the recording industry who agreed, they decided that their next serious project had to be recorded differently.

The Imani Winds in their latest recording project researched several engineers, looking for someone who was making recordings in the classical music scene. They listened to other chamber ensembles' recordings and sought names of engineers in the area making recordings they liked. Once they had found some professionals to talk to, The Imani Winds asked them to listen to their demo CD, and they in turn listened for reactions and suggestions that sounded "right" for recording their ensemble's next CD. "We decided that we wanted straight two-track recording with no mixing, and we knew that we would need really good mics," says Monica.

On the Technical Side of Things

You should use technology suited to classical music. Musicians are often intimidated by technology, and therefore will refuse to learn anything about it for fear that it will take away from the artistry. But, as David Finckel of the Emerson String Quartet says, you must see the entire recording project through yourself. He said in a recent interview for Chamber Music magazine, "We think it makes us play better to be involved." Being involved mandates a working knowledge of recording technology.

The microphones. The choice of microphones, according to Mays, will be the most critical technical decision for capturing your "performance". According to Rich Mays, some good mics for recording classical music are Neumann, Schoeps, and DPA (formerly B&K). Mays asserts that a single pair of mics is all one needs.

Two track recording. For the most part, only record onto two tracks. Mays says red flags should go up if a recording producer starts talking about multiple tracks and several microphones. Not only is this simpler method preferred by most classical music recording engineers, it is also less expensive.

Using a Producer

Many artists find it helpful to have another set of ears in the recording process besides the engineer. Monica Ellis describes having a producer for the Imani Winds' latest recording project as something that was vital to their recording. "Time is money," says Monica, and they didn't want to waste any by having to schedule another recording session to re-record a performance with which they weren't satisfied. The ensemble wanted to find someone to ensure that they made the best use of their time. "We wanted someone who is meticulous and excited about the music. There would be times when we'd play a take and think that it was fine, but [our producer] would tell us, 'let's try another one or two' and sure enough in listening for editing, the other takes were inevitably the ones we'd use." A producer can be a motivator, a good judge of your best sound (if he/she knows your playing), and an outside gauge for consistent quality interpretation of the music (if he/she knows the music you are playing). A professional producer can also take care of the variety of arrangements from the technical end, allowing you to spend more time thinking about making music. Judy Sherman, an admired record producer in New York, says that a producer must know your playing, have a concept of your particular sound, and also know the score. The person that oversees your session must have a sense of how things will come together and "have a sense of push and pull ... knowing when to get the bullwhip out and when to get out the silk gloves."

Editing

It is unrealistic to think that your recording will require no editing. Your recording engineer should know how to edit classical music. Otherwise, you'll subsequently end up hiring someone to edit and master it, which will significantly increase your costs. Once you've laid down high-quality recorded tracks, your recording should be edited in a way that maximizes that quality. You should be sure that your playing throughout the session isn't hindered by irregularities in playing due to fatigue or poor planning in rehearsal. You'll need consistent quality the whole time you are playing to put together an edited version of your music. Essential to listen for in editing: is the music coming through the speakers?

It may be that you will need or want to hire someone to master your recording; that is, take the edited master and refine it, including noise removal, fades, and other sound enhancements. This step is not always necessary. Some edited masters are very good and your recording engineer can polish the recording to high standards. Mastering can clean up room and lighting noise (which will most likely be present) and subtly enhance the recorded material. Keep in mind that the person who masters your recording must know classical music intimately, or the whole project can be wrecked.

In the Studio

Have a complete game plan in mind for your recording session.

Be prepared to spend some time at the beginning of the recording session getting to know the room and allowing the engineer to hear you in the room. You'll want to play various parts of your intended program to set levels for the recording. (Once levels are set, you'll not want to fuss with them.) Determine among your repertoire the moments with the fullest and loudest playing/singing and the moments of quiet.

Contemplate the order in which you'll play your pieces. Mays suggests starting with something easy and following that with the most difficult piece in your repertoire for the recording. You will get tired, so it's best not to put off the most technically challenging piece until you're exhausted. Concentrated recording time is tiring. Planning on spending more than three hours in a studio during one session is probably futile. You'll want your creative juices to flow freely when making your recording. Staleness and mistakes will only result in disappointment and cost you money. "Different people have different thresholds of tiredness," relates Monica Ellis. "We didn't know what ours were until we got into the studio." In making your recording, it will be important to allow for breaks to rest your body and your ears.

Mays advises that for every forty-five minutes of recording, you will get ten minutes of finished material. Don't expect to book a three-hour recording session and record a full-length sixty-minute CD. Finding out at the end of your allotted session that you've not recorded enough music will be very expensive.

Costs

Often, the money required to make a CD will come from your own pocket. Your group may choose to invest the fees from a few engagements to finance this kind of project, as did the Imani Winds for a recent recording. Sometimes you will luck into earmarked funds for this purpose; winning certain competitions might help you put together enough money to defray some or all of the production costs, for example. There are also grants specifically for this purpose, though admittedly not very many, and sometimes a private patron or other individual or institution might help with a targeted gift. (See Chapter VI, the section on "Patrons" for some examples and suggestions.)

You will need to devote a great deal of energy and focus to producing a good recording. You will need to be organized and careful to make sure that your money, time and other resources (including personnel) are used wisely.

The package for your CD isn't insignificant; you will want the packaging to reflect the musical intent of the recording. You will need to oversee this aspect of your project, making sure that if you are working with a recording company, a designer, someone writing liner notes, or other "outsiders" involved with the project, their vision is consistent with yours. Below, find a rough cost estimate for producing a commercial-quality CD (from start to finish):

Sample Budget (Three-Day Recording Session)*
*not including compensation of musical personnel

Recording Venue	$900
Equipment Rental	$650
Engineer	$2,500
Editing Time (in studio)	$750
Producer	$1,500
Duplication (1500 copies)	$1,000
Package Design and Printing	$1,500
Total	**$8,800**

Yes, making a recording can be expensive, and as Rich Mays says, "You're not going to want to have to make excuses when sending out your recording." Statements like, "Mr. Presenter? Yeah, well, um, we sound much better in person … trust me!" will not make the best impression to that potential employer.

But hopefully you've not thrown the towel in altogether on the idea of making a recording after reviewing these numbers. Read on:

Some Tips to Keep Costs Down

Talk with your engineer. Get clear ideas of capabilities and costs. Your engineer will be able to review different options and possibilities for saving money. A basic, good recording will most likely not come cheap.

Make your recording right on the front end. If your recording requires a lot of doctoring in the editing room, you'll have to **pay** someone to fix it (if it's even salvageable).

Are you in school? Record producer Judy Sherman suggests that many music schools and conservatories have recording services. If you are enrolled in a school with good facilities and the right technology, you might be able to make a recording for considerably less than in the professional world.

Bartering. Judy Sherman also reports success with bartering, trading services without the exchange of money. For instance, as an artist or ensemble you might offer a no-cost concert in exchange for using a particular facility's performance hall to record your CD. There are a variety of possibilities for creative exchanges of services.

Making a Recording on a Small Budget

A young oboe player that we know recently made a chamber music CD, including two major works, for about $800. For logistical reasons he had to use two venues, one for each of the works he was recording. As an alumnus of a major conservatory, he was able to use their hall and engineer for four hours for a total fee of $250, including the resulting CD itself; for the other half of the recording he rented equipment (mics, pre-amp and DAT machine) for $250, and used a friend's studio to record in. He paid an engineer $300 to do a few edits and put everything together. The only other cost was dinner and some wine for the colleagues who'd volunteered their services to play with him.

Our friend had looked into alternative arrangements, in case things with his school or with his friend's space hadn't worked out. He found a very nice church which would have cost $250 to rent for five hours, and a very well-established engineer, who works regularly with one of New York's major classical concert venues, who would have provided engineering services for the session, edited the recording (up to ten edits from a marked score) and handed him a CD for $600.

So, it's possible. Obviously, this didn't include packaging, extensive editing, or any bells and whistles, and wouldn't be a recording that one would plan to sell; but it was professional and clean, and reflected the young player's music making accurately.

Distributing Your CD

The Major-Label Industry as It Stands Now

Much of what one reads these days about classical music recording is a doomsday prophecy about the industry. Terry Teachout, in an article in the journal *Commentary*, writes that most labels have either all but abandoned any new classical music issues, or have confined new releases to reissues of recordings from an earlier decade. In fact, according to Teachout, in the last twenty years, CD reissues of performers recorded in the 1950's became the preferred choice of collectors compared to the more expensive new releases by younger artists. As reported in a recent issue of *Chamber Music* magazine, "Classical music on disc has lost nearly one-fifth of its business, accounting for just 1.8% of the total market."

In the past, recordings have often played a crucial role in creating musical celebrities, augmenting – or even surpassing – the role of live performance in launching and sustaining careers. The chances of this happening on a regular basis now are slim. Teachout doubts that few musicians under the age of forty will have the opportunity to record standard repertoire in a recording project on a major label. Naxos, which has studios in Nashville, Tennessee, is the only label now releasing recordings featuring new artists playing standard repertoire in any significant numbers; however, the releases are entirely repertoire driven, and it is unlikely that a specific artist will achieve stardom based on these projects. (Also, since Naxos compensates its artists with flat fees and artists receive no royalties, the artist doesn't make a lot of money – even if the disc is very successful.)

The Future of Selling Recordings

Several symphony orchestras, noted chamber ensembles and individual artists have begun recording on self-produced labels, distributing their recordings over the Web, at concerts, through advertisements in trade magazines, and by other means. Many artists seek funding from other sources to help them produce recordings, from foundation or private sources; alternatively, some seek out independent labels that, though far less widely distributed than major labels, are more open to taking on interesting projects, though sometimes with the artist assuming their own marketing costs. Many in the industry, including Ralph Jackson, President of the BMI Foundation, predict that this is where the future of the classical music recording industry lies. Self-produced recordings have the potential to strengthen artists' careers, by helping them to create a base of loyal fans.

The Internet has created the potential for an increased awareness of new music, young artists, new musical possibilities for the public and new musical products – and opportunities – for vendors. The Internet has made it much easier for smaller and non-profit record labels and for individuals to distribute their CDs; once downloading is widely available, predicts Teachout, it is possible that production costs will be greatly reduced, and artists may begin to see profits from self-produced recordings, something which only rarely happens now.

Marketing Your CD

In an interview in the *San Francisco Gate* on July 15, 2002, Rene Goiffon, president of Harmonia Mundi, states that while the pop industry successfully pairs recordings with public appearances, most classical CD releases "are not connected in any way … to musical life and concerts and so on." He cites this as one reason for the decline in classical music recording sales. As a young performer, you should make sure that your CD has a direct and specific connection to your musical life, interests, strengths and knowledge. Since you'll rely on your own expertise to produce this CD, it is essential that you release a recording that reflects at least one facet of who you are as a musician. If you plan on selling these recordings at your concerts or pitching a recital to a presenter, you may want to include the specific repertoire that you will be playing.

Beyond this, in order to get your CD noticed, you should keep two things in mind:

- The content of the recording should fill a niche, either with new repertoire or by featuring a unique approach to more standard repertoire.

- You should be willing to, and enthusiastic about, educating the public about the project, both the repertoire and the performance – the history of the music, the making of the recording, any other surrounding information that could enlighten and engage your listeners – in order to effectively sell it when it's produced.

Foster Reed and partner Tom Welsh manage and produce records for the experimental music label New Albion. In a July 16, 2002 interview, the reporter notes that the two spend as much time marketing CDs as producing them. Pitching a recording to a record store can be difficult. Reed says, "… chains tend to buy through a central buyer, so that potential enthusiasm [that an independent record store might have] is already structurally not present." New Albion does campaign for shelf space in the stores, but also sells CDs on the Internet.

The Internet and Recordings

The internet can be a way to efficiently and effectively promote and distribute recordings. Having the ability to get your music heard and seen on-line, through MP3 (a popular audio file format on the Internet) and similar technologies, provides the artist with immediate exposure. Lyn Liston, New Music Information Specialist for the American Music Center, says, "With people who make decisions [about programming and presenting], interest lasts briefly. Get them while there is that spark of interest. Then you have a chance of grabbing their attention." Being able to hear your work by downloading it from the Web – without waiting or bothering to request a recording – allows you to capture that interest and allows the consumer to make an instantaneous evaluation.

Also, a self-produced recording requires publicity, and even if your CDs are on record store shelves, the internet can help you with promotion. It can give you an opportunity to market your CD in the light of your artistic vision, to put your own "spin" on the material and provide a context for it.

Ralph Jackson of BMI predicts the continued formation of companies that maintain websites that contain a library of "house" recordings available for download and purchase. These websites allow web surfers to find categories of music or types of artists, and to assist them in finding quality recordings. Artists should inspect these websites; the New Music Jukebox, launched by the American Music Center, is one such site, where composers can make scores and recordings available for download and, eventually, purchase. Sites that put up downloadable recordings sometimes offer compensation to the artist based on the number of downloads, and some sites will even produce your recording and package it, receiving a share of the profits when it sells.

IV. Creating a Presence on the Internet

Why have a web page?

"Visit us on the Web!" is a phrase used for everything from magazines to shoe stores. Enormous numbers of people do visit the Web, and use it to do research, to communicate, and to make purchases. A website is active 24 hours a day, seven days a week. It allows people to read about you (reviews, quotes, biography), hear samples of your music, and see pictures of you, even when you yourself are not reachable. It lends credibility to your (forgive the expression) image, clarifies your artistic goals for the public, and makes them visible to a wide audience.

A website is also a very cost effective way of sharing information. Distributing this information becomes as easy as a couple of clicks, and updating it is, relatively, a piece of cake – not requiring the time and money for reprinting brochures, for example. "Presenters are always complaining that they never receive program notes, photos, bios and other stuff for a concert," says Steve Rosenthal of the Amherst Saxophone Quartet and designer of the group's website. "The website can provide these items to the concert presenter immediately." Bill Zukof of the ensemble Western Wind agrees, and adds that (as we've noted earlier) you will also have an effective way to sell independently produced recordings. Even if your CD isn't on the shelves of Barnes & Noble, it will be available in your own "corner store."

Will you become rich and famous from your web page? Probably not. What should you expect from having one? "Nothing ...," says Steve Rosenthal. "No one thing will make a huge difference. The only way to succeed is to do *everything* ... and keep doing it." Publishing a website with information about you or your ensemble will require continuous work to keep the site current, interesting and communicative. Basically, what you'll get from a well-designed website is a respectable promotional tool, which will hopefully enable you to keep in touch with an audience for your music.

Deciding what your website should be

What is your goal? What do you want to communicate? "Your message must be carefully thought out," says Steve Rosenthal. "No one is going to go to your website by accident."

Consider who's going to come to your website and what they are looking for. Rosenthal notes that it's rare, if ever, that a presenter will search the web to find artists for his/her series. What the web can actually do, in his opinion, is to help cultivate a loyal audience, which will be a selling point when you do get an engagement: "You can use the website to talk directly to audience members ... make contact with these people.. educate the public." Bill Zukof uses his group's website to talk to audiences by advertising and registering participants in the ensemble's educational workshops, and by including tour diaries to give fans notice and information about upcoming events. Establishing this kind of connection with an audience is of paramount importance.

While it may be rare that a presenter searches the web to find a musician for his/her series, it is not unlikely that a web surfer might stumble across your website in search of information, education, or simply while having fun browsing. You can use ancillary information included in your site to attract browsers who would not otherwise find you: information about the music you play, for example. Rosenthal's inclusion of information about saxophone literature on the Amherst Saxophone Quartet's website attracts many more hits than the ensemble alone would attract. As web surfers worldwide consult your website for information, they also learn about you. Rosenthal estimates that he receives over 1,200 "hits" on the ensemble's site each month; that's a lot of people learning about the Quartet!

"Great," you say. "I've got some stuff I can put up on the web. There's that picture of me and my grandma at my senior recital, and I'll put up my paper I wrote for Fishborn's Romantic History class." Obviously, creating an unprofessional, poorly produced website could be worse than not having one at all. Your web presence must reflect the look and feel of your other materials (all of which are, of course, very well done).

Putting it all together

To get some ideas, look at other websites and ask yourself, "What about his site do I like/dislike, and what is effective (or not) about this communication?" You will want to come up with a list of elements that are within your reach and supportive of your goals. Remember the unique capabilities of the Internet: interactivity, the ability to present recorded excerpts of your playing, frequent updating, among others.

Creating a Web page

Whether you hire someone to create your page or create one yourself, Steve Rosenthal suggests that you should learn some simple HTML, the code used to program web sites. HTML programming is too easy not to know something about. (Rosenthal says that the creating part of web design is easy; the hard part is marketing.) Knowing basic HTML will allow you to update information as your career develops without constantly having to consult your web designer.

To design your page, if you choose to do it yourself, you can use a program like FrontPage, Microsoft Word, Adobe InDesign, or Dream Weaver, end-user software programs designed to help you create web pages by simplifying keystrokes and programming language commands. You'll need to know something about basic graphic design principles so that you can clearly communicate the goal for your website. "Most people think that graphic design is about making things looks good," says Steve Rosenthal, "It's not. It's about communicating as clearly as possible." With a little artistic panache and specific goals, you can create an operational, unique campaign for your music making.

Okay, so you know some basic programming code, you've read "Design for Dummies," but you want your creation designed by a professional. You can have your website designed by an expert. Costs vary for professional web design, but usually start at $1000 and can easily reach $3,000 to $4,000. It's possible that you'll be able to corral an experienced friend or colleague into helping you set up your site for a much lower cost than a specialized professional web-design team. Unless you're made of money, you'll want the construction of your website to allow for updates to the copy. Set up the site so that as you announce concert dates and obtain reviews, **you** can insert new text and remove the old.

You will also need to obtain a place to put your site, or a host. If you are in or associated with a school, many offer free or low cost web site hosting. Also, commercial providers like AOL, Earthlink, and CompuServe offer free site hosting with an account, but the space is limited. There are low to no cost options with other companies if you display what are known as banner ads-- commercial space you provide to other companies for free web site hosting. On the low-budget end of things or while your web site is in its creative stages, you can save your page as an HTML file and email it to others. Both Internet Explorer and Netscape can view HTML documents as files. On the other end of the spectrum, you might consider purchasing your own domain name. This option probably projects the most professional image and will add consistency for years to come when per chance you'll change Internet Service Providors or graduate from school. You can purchase web-hosting services for as little as $20 per month.

Important Elements of a Web Site

First and foremost, the site should have a feel that makes sense to the user and is easily navigable, so that those who visit not only can find the information they seek but are inspired to look further. Rosenthal suggested, "After you've created you masterpiece, watch 200 people use it. If they can't find something [easily on your website], then it's not their fault." (Maybe only 50, or even 25 people can be your test group for this!) The front page should not be cluttered, should contain only a screen's-worth (Zukof's words) of information, and should communicate your goal from the very beginning.

Consistency makes the difference between a professional looking website and an amateur one. Design elements should have a coherent feel, and you want the atmosphere to establish your identity – and to make it memorable.

You must show your name and contact information on every page of the website; no matter what page of the site a surfer is visiting, you want her to know that she has YOU to thank for the information, and this it is YOU to whom she should look for further information.

Be sure to view your site with multiple browsers to make sure that you've created a page that is compatible with multiple computer platforms. (Many people still use the original, old versions of Netscape or Internet Explorer that came with their computer. Also, consider other browsers with which people might try to view your site like Unix-based or Palm-based web browsers.). Your site should be universally accessible to viewers with various screen sizes and speeds of Internet connections. Lots of images and flash programs (animation software used to create interactive graphics) on your page will be more difficult to view with a slow Internet connection.

How will others find your website in the sea of others? Make sure that your site is listed with major search engines. You might initially try performing a search in several engines to see what comes up in your genre of music, your instrument, and even you or your ensemble's name. You'll want to distinguish your website so that it is clear and appealing. A listing in many search engines will occur inevitably as *spider programs*, automated programs designed to collect information from the Web, index your new site in the ever-growing branches of the Internet. Steve Rosenthal reminds potential website creators of a secret of the trade: creating metatags so that your site is properly listed with search engines who use *spider programs*. Metatags are words you place in the HTML code after the header that many search engines use as keywords for search techniques. Be sure to include misspellings of words and important words that describe your website.

When you've created your website, it should be a creation that operates to advance your visibility and communication ability. Publicizing your site only on search engines isn't enough. Make sure your URL, or your Web address, is on business cards, letterhead, brochures, and your voice mail. Now that you've spent all of this time creating it, you should share it with as many people possible. Radio broadcasts of performances of Western Wind on NPR always include a "for more information…" clause that tells listeners about their website.

Keep your site current with dates, new developments, reviews, and other events. Bill Zukof says that his audience gets impatient if the Western Wind website is not updated on a regular basis. Audiences look for "new" and "updated" additions to websites. Since updating your website will not require the additional costs as would be incurred in reprinting a flyer, keep your audience regularly informed. If you have exciting information, one way to share it is through your Web presence – be it through an updated link or email newsletter. Changes to your website reflect the burgeoning direction of your career. The magnificence of the Internet is interactivity. Your website is your chance to network with your audience outside of the concert hall.

V. Assembling Credentials

Before anyone will hire you to do something, you have to have done something. In order to make yourself appealing to a presenter, you have to have some negotiable credentials, in the form of performance experience, competition wins, or other evidence of your level of accomplishment. In this chapter we'll deal with competitions and self-produced concerts; for more advice on getting performances, see Chapter VIII, part 2, "Self-Management."

Competitions

The great number of music competitions indicates, among other things, that consumers in the field are most comfortable with easily identified testimonials which validate a performer's expertise. Competitions seem to provide this by applying objective, recognized and respected standards to the selection process.

The problem is that music competitions are not like sports competitions. There may be someone who can run the fastest, or someone who can be described as the best tennis player in the world, at least for a brief time, but there simply isn't someone who is THE BEST at playing the *Brahms Second Piano Concerto*. The standards by which music competitions are judged are, thankfully, subject to human sensibility rather than to quantifiable criteria. But this means that they are also subject to inequities and frustrations.[1] Nonetheless, the general public, and even professionals in the field, often behave as if winning a given competition actually means that the winners are THE BEST, and pay them attention accordingly. Which adds to the general disgruntlement.

---

[1] The problems and irritations of competitions are too frequently discussed and complained about to spend many words on, but to let you know that we know about them (and sympathize) we will mention only that they can be restrictive, biased, unimaginative and unpleasant.

In spite of which you will probably do some competing at some point, perhaps because in a crowded field, with limited opportunities, you need to get someone's attention. *Competitions are one way - not the only way, but a way which is available to most everyone - to get someone's attention. Perhaps just about everyone's attention, for a minute.*

Certainly competitions can be an important part of a performer's career building (for some individuals, the most important part). Doing well in a particular competition or audition may sometimes be necessary in order to reach a particular goal. Some benefits which can come out of competitions are:

• Opportunities for those not well-connected in the field to develop some important connections

• Opportunities to hear other emerging musicians perform; opportunities to be heard, by one's peers as well as by judges; and the chance to broaden your peer group, talk with colleagues about the field, learn about other opportunities, and get comments or input

• The chance to begin to define what you do best, what you do well, and to learn how you perform under stress

• Performance experience

These are all benefits which can be obtained from competitions, win or lose, if you know how to go about getting them. If you win, of course, you can add to these:

• Cash and other valuable prizes, including performances

• Public recognition and attention

• Something to fill out your biographical materials

What no competition ever is:

• An instant career.

We will address some possible benefits individually, and provide some guidance about how best to obtain them; however, you need to think about how to find out what competitions exist, and how to pick which ones to enter.

Where are they? What are they?

We assume that you know about the competitions closest to you, those run by your school while you're still enrolled. As for all the others, performers often find out about them in a hit-or-miss fashion, either through word of mouth from colleagues, teachers and others, or by seeing a notice on a bulletin board somewhere. This method may work reasonably well, but probably isn't the most efficient way to plan your time and allocate the money and effort you'll put into competing. Some more organized research is in order. The best single source is the *Guide to Competitions*, published annually by Concert Artists Guild. The *Guide* is cross referenced by category and location. The annual *Musical America International Directory* has an extensive listing of competitions including many for performers. Most colleges and universities, and all conservatories, maintain a listing of competitions for their students' (and often their alumni's) use.

In addition, many orchestras have competitions for which the prize is a concerto performance. Often, these kinds of competitions will be aimed at younger or local artists, and you can inquire with the orchestras you think are likely to hold them in your area. Music teachers' organizations often sponsor competitions, as do instrument-specific societies. A bit of detective work can ferret out competitions which will be useful to you. Don't neglect your local papers as a source of this information. For younger artists, competitions which offer scholarships or other similar prizes are often announced through the local paper, and major city newspapers will occasionally print deadline information about the major international competitions.

Which competitions to enter

Participating in competitions, as stated above, can require a significant investment of time, effort, and money. Therefore, your choice of which competitions to enter should be informed by reasonable and specific goals. Looking through lists of past winners of any competition, including the biggest and most prestigious, should convince you that the winners, overall, have by no means been guaranteed a wildly successful future. Conversely, among today's most famous young solo artists, a good number have never won any competitions - or entered any, to our knowledge - but have gotten onto the "major career" track by a completely different route.

Goals should be as specific as possible, and should match what the competition offers as a prize and how the competition is run. For example, if your goal is to gain experience in performing with an orchestra, you might enter one of the orchestra-run concerto competitions which are held all over the country. If your goal is to be heard by some important musicians in your field, a competition that has several rounds, at least some of them live where many judges will hear you, is the right one for you. Your goal can be solely mercenary (entering because you need the prize money is legitimate), or just wanting to know how colleagues outside your normal sphere of activity like your playing. You can have several goals; the important point is that they be specific (so that you can evaluate whether you've achieved them) and realistic (so that you don't waste valuable resources).

In choosing which competitions to enter, the rule of thumb should be as follows:

You hope to win, and believe that it's realistically possible for you to do so, so you should want and be ready for the prize when you do.

This means that the competition should 1) be appropriate for your level of performance and experience; and 2) match your musical strengths.

The major international competitions, for example, may well include very extensive concert tours - 100 or so dates in a year - as part of the prize package. If you've never performed more than three or four times during a season, and have not done much (or any) touring, you're unlikely to have the stamina that such a schedule requires. Also, some of the 100 concerts will be in major halls, in situations where you will be judged by the same standards as any of the other artists, seasoned professionals, who regularly play there. No matter how gifted, you may find yourself prematurely facing the world's most critical public.

Similarly, if you enter a contemporary music performance competition and you dislike contemporary music, you're certainly unlikely to win, but also - if by some chance you do - you're unlikely to be able to take advantage of the performance and networking opportunities which will arise from it.

Aside from the clearly stated mission of the competition, it is possible to get some insight into the kind of artist that a given competition is looking for by learning something about its recent winners. If you consider all the winners of a given competition over the past five years to be colorless, middle-of-the-road, boring performers, and you think of yourself as outrageous, iconoclastic and absolutely unlike anyone they've chosen, you may in fact be at a disadvantage in this one. Of course, you may be determined to become the X competition's first artist-winner of any interest, and if so, it's worth a try.

Once you have a clear idea of which competitions you might want to enter, start to think about scheduling. Since traveling to competitions outside your immediate location requires money (for transportation, lodging, food, practice time and more, certainly for yourself and sometimes for an accompanist as well), and since preparing repertoire requires great care and effort in all cases, it's wise to carefully budget these resources. Try to do several competitions which allow you to overlap or repeat repertoire within a season, rather than simply doing one a year. (Given the age limits most competitions have, you won't be able to do very many if you do one a year anyway.) If you've traveled, say to Europe, to enter a competition, see if you can build yourself a small competition circuit. Winning a prize in one or some of them may help to pay for the trip, more people will have heard you perform, you'll get more mileage and experience with the repertoire you've learned, and you'll begin to gain smoothness and confidence in your auditioning ability as you go along.

Don't try, however, to do more than you can take on and still do well. It's not useful to do a bad audition, and you're creating perfect conditions for performing poorly by being exhausted or distracted. Artists in our competition have been known to travel back and forth between our semi-final and final rounds and the equivalent rounds of another competition in some far away city; none of these musicians has won ours, nor have they won the others, to our knowledge. There are always exceptions, of course, and you know your own stamina and ability to perform under stress better than we could. (One singer, who won a first prize in our competition a number of years ago, knocked the socks off the judges in spite of having just walked off an all-night flight from China at the end of an opera tour.) Still, think about this before plunging in.

Build in time during the circuit schedule to allow for sufficient rehearsal with accompanists, if you're not going to be working with the same one for all your auditions.

One last thing to consider when doing your selecting and scheduling is to try to allow time during and after each competition to take advantage of the professional and social opportunities that will almost certainly be a part of winning, and which may well be a part of simply participating in, the competition. The competition administration can give you an idea of what will be happening; whether you can attend auditions by other artists, for example, or receptions with your fellow competitors, judges, patrons of the competition and the press, and - should you win - whether you should be available for any special events. More about this further along in this section.

The following ideas are dispatches from the field, advice based on the collective experience of our friends on the competition circuit, and on our own experience of who does well in our competition, and how.

Choosing repertoire

Some competitions have required repertoire which you will have to prepare; others have some required works or categories of works; still others have no requirements at all, and may consider your ability to create interesting programs part of their evaluation of you as an artist. Whatever you do,

DON'T BASE YOUR REPERTOIRE DECISIONS ON
AN ATTEMPT TO OUTGUESS THE JUDGES.

It is far better to impress with what you can do than to dutifully perform something you think you should. To whatever degree you have any flexibility, choose repertoire which emphasizes your strengths and individuality as an artist. If you are given a great deal of freedom, remember that a competition program should almost never be a conservatory graduation program. You may need to demonstrate your versatility and breadth of musicianship, but you don't have to show that you can play particular works in order to do so. Also, don't try to play the way you think the judges will want you to; play your own way, which is the only way you can really be consistently convincing.

Frustratingly, both of the following are true:

War horses, certainly the greatest and best known of them, can be dangerous, and a jury will almost certainly have specific ideas about exactly how a well-known work should be played. Also, they may have heard the work twelve times just before your turn comes up.

On the other hand, a program of completely unusual and unfamiliar works, unless you're a specialist in a certain area, can make a jury uneasy about their ability to judge your performance.

So, there you are: the choice, ultimately, has to be determined by what you do best.

One other consideration. If you are an instrumentalist or singer who will be performing with an accompanist, and if the accompanist will be provided by the competition or is someone with whom you've not worked before, it's obvious but important to remember to take into account the ensemble difficulties of the works you're programming. Don't provide yourself with an additional and unnecessary challenge when there are so many you have to deal with already.

If you are working with an accompanist that you provide, the pianist should be absolutely excellent. The quality of your musical collaboration, and your musical judgment in picking someone with whom to collaborate, will (or should) be a factor in assessing your performance. And working with a fine musician will require - and inspire - you to do your best.

Program order

This is the same story. Many competitions allow you to start with a selection of your own choosing. Play to strength; start with what you do best, and what makes you comfortable and relaxed. Don't choose a work to start in which there's a danger that you may completely self-destruct, even if it's a sure dazzler when you hit it just right. If it's that impressive, the judges will likely ask for it later, when you're apt to be more caught up in the flow of the performance.

On-stage presentation

The stage director and performance coach, Janet Bookspan, sums up how to make the best of the audition situation as follows: "There are no auditions, there are only performances." This is probably the best single piece of advice on the topic we've encountered. Granted, an audition can often be a weird sort of performance, where your audience may be entitled to interrupt you at will, where you don't always know exactly what you will play, and during which you may not be able to see or hear the people to whom you're playing. Nonetheless, if you are able to maintain the integrity of the "performance," thinking of the piece from beginning to end and wanting to share your performance with your listeners, you're much more likely to draw them into your experience and convince them of your musical vision.

In addition to your actual performance of the music, the "no auditions, only performances" idea means that the etiquette of performing remains, modified, of course, according to the specific situation. If there's no actual audience but only a small judging panel (or just one judge), you probably shouldn't bow when you take the stage, but a gracious smile as you enter, and an equally gracious acknowledgment - plus a thank you - when you leave are essential. (Since smiling also actually is a tension reliever, it can help with performance nerves.)

Dress: for the weather, which may mean that you have to be comfortable rather than glamorous, and for the occasion, which means finding out as much as possible about what the occasion is, and what is the suggested level of formality. As always, ask for information.

Memorization

Certainly do memorize your music if you can. Singers and pianists almost always have their music memorized; string players usually do if it's a concerto, and usually don't if it's a sonata; wind players and others often don't, but should. There is widespread feeling that a sonata, played by an instrumentalist with piano, should not be memorized, backed up by either "tradition" or a desire to not make the pianist look less like an equal partner. In our opinion (and we realize that this is a minority view), this is silly. It would be nice if the pianist would also memorize the music, but we're a long way from that; meanwhile, the less there is to come between performer and listener, the better. The performer's eyes fixed on the music, and even the presence of a music stand, can quite effectively create a barrier to communication. If you must use music and a stand, position it so that it can be ignored by the listener, and don't allow yourself to stare at the pages. (This last advice applies equally to actual performances, not just to auditions.)

Attitude

We've often felt that before musicians enter competitions, it would be great if they could judge several of them. Judging is a difficult process, challenging in both musical and emotional ways; some judges find themselves on firm ground with the former, and yet uncomfortable with the latter. Though they may feel that it's inappropriate to express any direct reaction to your performance, the judges almost always want to like you. There is nothing more exciting for a competition judge than to be overwhelmed with wonderful performances, even if that means more difficult challenges in making their decisions. Assume that even if the physical circumstances make a particular audition less than comfortable, the goodwill and sympathy are there. Such an attitude can never hurt, and may well help you to create the most positive impression possible.

If you don't win

Not winning can mean everything from not even getting through a first round to getting second prize. Assuming you performed at all creditably,

DON'T:

Slink off, and try and forget the whole thing as quickly as possible;

DO:

Try and squeeze every last possible benefit out of the competition before you pack your things and head home.

Among the things you can certainly do:

• If you have been eliminated, try to attend the auditions by your peers. You'll learn a lot about who's out there in the field, about repertoire, and about the subtle factors in performance technique that influence juries. It certainly will be interesting, both musically and otherwise. You may have a chance to meet and talk with people involved with the competition; administrators, judges, colleagues, patrons, press. Even when the auditions are technically closed, the powers-that-be might let you attend with special permission. Of course, if you're still an active participant, don't do this; it would probably be both inappropriate, and is likely to be disturbing to your own concentration to listen to everyone else's performances.

• Attend any social or press events which are scheduled in association with the competition, for the networking reasons stated above.

• Try to get as much feedback as you possibly can about whether anyone who heard you liked your work. In addition to the judges, there might have been others - managers, teachers, conductors, composers, presenters, patrons, press - who attended the auditions. If any of them, including the judges, were interested in you, they might be willing to give you advice or other help. We've known performers in our and other competitions who didn't win, including some who didn't even get past the preliminary tape round, who were able to find a teacher, gain scholarship assistance, get performance engagements and financial help with special projects and establish important ongoing friendships, by simply making sure they met and spoke to as many sympathetic people as they could. The competition administration should advise you as to what is appropriate and when to back off gracefully. It's good etiquette to ask the administration's advice in approaching judges and others.

• If you do well, make sure that someone knows about it. Your hometown newspapers will certainly be interested if you place among the top winners, as might such publications as your alumni newsletter. Send out a letter or press release.

When you win

The advice for what to do when you win a competition is, surprisingly, much like that offered for when you don't. The difference is that the possible opportunities for learning, networking, and publicity outlined above become certain opportunities when you've been chosen as a winner. You're now the star. There will almost certainly be social events; go to them. There will certainly be people who were impressed with your performance; meet them, learn about them, and add them to your mailing list. In addition, make sure the people who have been interested in or have even supported your career up to this point learn of the victory, and that you thank them for their part in your success. Learn about the competition's public relations efforts on your behalf, and find out if you can help them by being prepared with photos, bios and the like. If the competition is a very major one, they will almost certainly be doing equally major publicity for you. Nonetheless, get on the phone yourself, and see whether the excitement surrounding the win can turn possibilities into realities. (If you've been doing well overall, and this is a major event in what could now be a major career push, seriously consider hiring a good publicist right away.) If a management firm has been looking at you, or if a concert series has been considering including you in their season, make sure they know about your triumph immediately.

Find out about what resources the competition has that they can use on your behalf, in addition to the specific prizes listed in the brochure. You shouldn't expect to learn all this instantly; rather, expect to find out gradually and gracefully. We've known artists who have won competitions and developed ongoing relationships with the administration and/or sponsors; these friends have sometimes provided assistance far beyond the amount of the original award. Actual examples, small and large, of these items include:

a tuxedo;
funding for a recording;
a London debut;
a collaboration with a well-known television star on a special project;
a generous living stipend for a year.

None of these was included in the prize the artists originally won. They were given later on, as the result of continued interest in the artist by people involved with the competition, combined with the artists keeping up contact and making their career development needs known.

A final word on competitions

Have some perspective, and be prepared for the fact that no one can please everyone, and that, though you may do marvelously at X competition they may not respond equally well at Y competition. Don't call the competition administration and yell at them for their bad taste. It won't help you any, except to relieve your feelings slightly; it probably won't hurt you either, since most competition administrators will not hold an angry phone call against you forever -but it might, and certainly isn't particularly polite.

Debuts ... and Alternatives

If one defines "debut" as a New York debut, and if the intention of the reader is to self-produce such an event, the advice is very short:

DON'T DO IT.

Here are some of the reasons.

The New York debut is something of a musical dinosaur, without the importance it may once have had. Having a New York debut under one's belt almost never makes any difference at all to one's career development. The phone will not ring the next morning with offers of management, engagements and the like. Almost certainly, **nothing will happen.**

There is only one newspaper in New York which has the staff, space and ongoing interest to try and regularly cover debut recitals: *The New York Times.*[2] And even they have limited numbers of critics, and a limited number of inches devoted to classical music reviews. If you're spending the vast amounts of money a debut can cost for the sake of a review, know that anything - a snow storm, illness, too many conflicting musical events, or, forgive us, a lack of interest in your event - can prevent you from getting one. Then, consider the likelihood of getting a good review with reprintable lines. (How often do you agree with the critic's assessment of a concert?) So much for the newspapers.

New York debuts can be fiercely expensive to produce. In addition to the hall costs, you must add in the extras: everything from the cost of a recital manager should you use one (perhaps $2,000), to advertising, accompanists or guest artists, travel, hotels and food (if you don't live in New York), and more. If you have the $5,000 to $15,000 such an event costs, there are better ways to spend the money, all of which are more likely to have a positive effect on your career.

---

[2] Note the word "try." Even *The Times* has changed its editorial policy, and doesn't particularly prioritize debut reviews when making assignments.

This isn't just our jaded view. Every year or so, newspapers in New York City write about the demise of the New York debut, often with some relief. As long ago as 1993, Alex Ross wrote an article with the headline, "The Debut: Grand Rite of Passage Now Passe" in *The Times*. He said, "The interesting question is ... whether this much respected ritual has become less significant in recent years? In an age of proliferating technology and information, this neat event - a private, solo debut in a New York concert hall - seems somewhat superfluous. Foreign artists more often make an impact on these shores first through the medium of recordings. Young artists can make their way to possible fame through competitions, auditions, radio broadcasts and select debut series." And later, "The very idea of a New York debut clings to memories of a time when the city revolved around the symphony, the opera, the recital. The rituals and institutions of classical music cannot shake nostalgia for a long-lost age of splendor and innocence. Young artists have discovered new, less cumbersome modes of establishing themselves and getting noticed: recordings, venturesome programming, involvement with new music." And since that article was written, the situation hasn't improved for debutants, so to speak.

Does this mean that one should never make a New York debut? No, since there are circumstances which would make doing so at least slightly more sensible. They include:

1. When someone else is paying. The best possible debut is one for which you receive a fee. If someone hires you to perform your New York debut as part of their "Great Artists" series or whatever, take it. If the debut is a competition prize, it has a greater chance of attracting some press interest. If it's the gift of a patron, and you can't convince this person to put the money into something more practical, it may or may not prove useful, but at least you're not risking your own money - which presumably is in short supply.

2. When your career has reached a stage where, in spite of significant exposure and serious credentials established in many other locations, you have not had and are not expecting an offer to perform in New York. Combined with the expectation that a particular group of important people will attend - critics who have been following your career outside of New York, managers, conductors, presenters, other influential musicians - and the potential for attracting a respectable audience (not entirely made up of friends and family), a self-produced debut might be worthwhile.

3. When you specifically need to have done a New York recital to get tenure at a teaching job. You should still try to get some outside source to pay, but an investment in your employment future is understandable. However, it would be still better to work within the system to move beyond this outdated benchmark of performance achievement; there are many other things a teacher can do to prove her stuff, and even to do some real good for the field in general.

4. You're not an individual but rather an ensemble, based in New York, and the debut is not really a debut but rather the first concert of an annual series. Many groups want to have an annual concert or concert series of their own in their home base, in which they can have artistic control, experiment with repertoire, and develop a home base following. If your home base is New York City, well, there you are. Whether or not it's New York, your group may - following rule number one above, that it's better to have someone else pay, at least in part - choose to follow the not-for-profit route, and may then apply to various funding sources to support these programs. (See Chapter XIII, "General Resources," for more of this information.)

A New York critic we know has pointed out, very sensibly, that the debuts he is most interested in are those which are scarcely debuts at all. These are concerts performed by artists who have been heard regularly, even frequently, in other situations, whether as guest artists on other programs, as part of a chamber ensemble, or as soloists in concerto programs. Also included in this category are artists who have developed a strong following outside of New York, and whose first performance in this city is an occasion of significant interest. These artists come before the public with a certain amount of credibility and reputation Not only do they attract somewhat more interest than would the average untested and unproven debut artist, the expectations may be more positive, and the general attitude toward them may be kinder, less "show me."

New York Debut Alternatives

If you think about what you would hope to get from doing a New York debut, you can probably achieve the same thing cheaper, and with greater potential for success, by other means. If your aim is to gather reviews, you have a much better chance of doing this by developing regional opportunities, either in your home location (more about this below) or in a variety of important locations around the country and abroad. For the same cost as a self-produced New York recital, you can produce recitals in two or three other cities where there are excellent papers and good halls. Your chances of getting press coverage are much improved; and, because you will be performing in several locations, your chances of getting exposure, creating a regional following, and doing other significant networking are greater as well.

Though many cities are rich in musical events, most are not as absolutely saturated as is New York. If your goals include accumulating credentials, the preceding advice holds true. If your goal is to test yourself in a major musical marketplace, the same again. In other words, think about self-produced performances as a career investment, and always be looking at any investment in a hard-headed way, with an eye on the payoff. Be specific about this. Know what you want, and think of how best to get it.

In thinking about what you want, realize that not all successful and fulfilling careers are national or international. Several artists we know have made fine, rewarding careers limited to their own city or region. In these locations they are in great demand, have loyal followings who wouldn't miss one of their concerts, and are both lauded and devotedly followed by the local critics. They work all the time, and have musically very fulfilling lives. In the section on the press, we describe how you will almost always have an advantage in your home town (as long as it's not New York) in attracting attention, so do remember this when considering where best to invest your financial and creative resources.

Always try and get someone else to produce the recital if you can. There are concert series in important cities around the country which produce debut recitals and pay a fee to the artists; it may not be much, but at least you won't have hall and related costs, there is usually a built in audience of non-relatives, and the fee may cover some of your other expenses. Some of these concerts are broadcast on the radio, and are that much more valuable as a result. Needless to say these opportunities are limited and highly competitive, but are worth trying for if you're ready for them.

There is one other avenue you may want to explore, if you are self-producing and don't want to come in completely as a new kid on the block. With sufficiently respectable credentials, you can approach the producer or presenter of an appropriate concert series (meaning a series which sometimes includes emerging or debut artists, or might do so, given a good reason), suggest that you have managed to raise the financial backing and would like to be considered for inclusion in the series. The producer / presenter may just possibly bite, since, if you are of any interest to them, you'll be saving them money on their overall season costs. No one but you and the producer need know that the arrangement is any different from that with any of their other featured artists. You will have the advantage of the built-in audience, critics who regularly attend these programs, and a more important showcase than you would be able to manage on your own.

About Recital Managers

You can hire someone to take care of all the nonmusical aspects of a self-produced event for you, for a fee. In New York, a recital manager will cost approximately $2,000 plus the expenses you would assume anyway (for postage, flyers, etc.), a fee which will generally cover the following services: writing and sending out press releases; arranging for the design, printing and mailing of flyers; helping to plan and place your advertising; sending out special invitations; working with the concert hall and arranging your rehearsal schedule there; assisting with your overall planning; and overseeing the event (and coping with last minute problems). They cannot guarantee reviews or feature stories preceding the concert, and if they say they will, they're probably not honest and you shouldn't hire them.

One other item which a recital manager can often take care of for you is hall "papering." Unless you have a massive number of friends and family in addition to the VIPs that you hope will attend, your hall might look a little forlorn with only a few folks in it. The answer for many artists is making tickets available at no charge to deserving groups - senior citizens, students, foreign visitors, and others. Though you can contact the appropriate centers yourself, it certainly is helpful to have your recital manager take care of this for you.

As to whom to hire, you should ask those who have done recitals at that location for recommendations. Shop around, be very choosy, and make an arrangement which clearly states everyone's responsibilities.

96

VI. Networking

"Few people are successful unless a lot of other people want them to be. "
- Author unknown

First, forget the idea that the music field is controlled by relatively few people, that those who have the work get the work, that success comes about through connections, power, and money, and that the entire structure exists (at least in part) to keep you out. Forget it not because it's not true, but because - except for the last part - it is. And not all the reasons for this are reprehensible.

In the first chapter of this book, we discussed how musicians are trying to find regular work and success in a buyer's market, and how the buyers generally like to work with those they know. You wouldn't pick a doctor out of the yellow pages (or after receiving a flyer in the mail), knowing that your health is at stake; neither does a presenter, or manager, or orchestra administrator want to hire performers without knowing a lot about them, when the health of their business is at stake. Realistically, even with the best will in the world and marvelously discriminating ears, these people can't listen to everyone.

Imagine, then, that the field is like a big room, and in it are all those who have the work, and wanting to get in are all those who don't - yet. Your job is to learn where all the doors into the room are, and what it takes to open them. Though staying in is often as difficult as getting in the first place, the approach to both is basically the same. One essential key is networking.

Networking is a term which describes making and understanding those relationships which nurture and sustain a career. No career, in any field, can exist without supportive networks.

If you graduate from Harvard Business School, you have more than a diploma and a well-respected credential with which to negotiate a good job. You have developed a group of potentially supportive peers and mentors, who may well turn into customers, providers of recommendations, sources of information - in other words, a "network" of invaluable contacts. All musicians need the same kind of network, and without it they can't effectively do business.

In this section of the book, we've identified several groups of individuals, from the constituencies noted in Chapter I, with whom forming ongoing relationships is both particularly important and yet not often discussed. There are other groups, equally important, which will be discussed in other sections of this book (managers and presenters, for example). Also, some groups should be obvious, and a brief look at one of them - your colleagues - should serve to introduce principles which will recur throughout each chapter.

If you have attended a conservatory or other music school, and/or have worked for a while in the field, you have almost certainly developed a network of colleagues who like you and your music making. They include your peers in and out of school, your teachers, and your mentors and advisors. They will often be the source - for many musicians, the primary or only source, throughout their lives - of most of the contacts with which you will build your career, as you will be for them. It is our assumption that the importance of making mutually supportive friendships is obvious.

This is perhaps the place to introduce your most important business tool, next to your instrument:

Your address book.

The reason for introducing it here is that, though we would not presume to teach you how to make friends, we can advise you on how to deal with your friends as professional colleagues. Even your friends appreciate thank you messages, written or by phone, for introductions or referrals made on your behalf. They also appreciate your making similar contacts on their behalf. They like being remembered on special occasions, or when they've had a musical success; they like being kept abreast of your activities. So, keep your address book correct and current, and write and call.

The person who is recommended for a job - or anything else - is often the person who has most recently been brought to memory. By remaining current with your colleagues you can be that person.

Your immediate colleagues are the most basic and obvious of your networking groups. Some groups that are not so obvious, whose role in the network is more complex than might be supposed, or that are just plain harder to get to know, follow.

Patrons

The ideas in this section are based largely on talks given at the Career Moves workshops by former CAG board president Leslie Christian, an extraordinary individual who has been a generous patron to both arts groups and individuals, and amazingly honest about her own motivations for giving. Additional important ideas have been provided by another former CAG board president, Edith Greenwood.

Here is a story which exemplifies many musicians' concept of an arts patron:

> Despairing, the musicians sit in the darkened theater, knowing that for lack of funds the concert will not go on. All looks bleak, when Mrs. Musiclover, world-famous patron of the arts, appears in the wings. "The show must go on. Here's my checkbook; name the figure," she announces. "The concert season is saved!" exclaim the musicians. General rejoicing.

If you share the common view of the subject, you assume that a patron of the arts is an extraordinarily wealthy individual who doles out lavish sums to a well-connected few – most of whom are less talented and less deserving than you would be. A community of especially well-heeled philanthropists does indeed exist; we all know the names of the most celebrated of the music patrons, as their last names are usually thought to be Hall, or Pavilion, or Space. They are regularly and tenaciously approached for assistance by all and sundry, since their interest in the field is at least known, and since - like most of the world - musicians are not very imaginative about investigating new possibilities, and have a particularly difficult time imagining why anyone, perhaps excepting these mysterious few people, would give their money away at all.

However, patrons aren't simply PATRONS; they are also patrons, individuals who are able and willing to lend various kinds of support to another person or project for a variety of reasons. You already have patrons within your existing network: friends and family who wouldn't miss one of your concerts, for example. They could, after all, make some excuse, and stay home and watch television - but they choose instead to attend and applaud, and sometimes bring their friends and even pay for their tickets. In other words, patronage involves a pattern of supportive assistance which can range from small commitments of time to large financial donations. It can include any or all of the following:

• **Physical presence at your events**

• **Getting the word out and networking on your behalf**

• **Contributions other than money**

• **And, yes, money**

Unless this range of patronage possibilities is understood, you will close off potential sources of support, pay too little attention to smaller patrons who may be just as valuable as larger ones (and who may turn into the latter at some point), and approach the development of this constituency in the wrong way. Don't just focus on the very rich. It's important to realize that those who can't give $25,000 to a project of yours but who could give $500 may be actually better suited to you. Donors of large sums may require famous recipients, whereas a younger or beginning philanthropist might identify more closely with you at your career stage.

Though you're almost certainly reading this chapter to learn about the people who can help you finance big projects, and not to learn how to remind people to come to your concerts, the former really can and does develop out of the latter. Developing a group of fans who can be counted on for various kinds of help means developing mutually satisfying and mutually beneficial relationships - and that takes years of careful cultivation.

If this notion of cultivating helpful people is upsetting or daunting, we remind you again to think in terms of building your business, not your art. You would be less wary about remembering and identifying people who might invest in your business than those who might invest in your career; however, there probably is little reason for your ambivalence and hesitation. There is great potential for mutual benefit to be gained from the investment, as will be discussed later in this chapter.

Know Your Customer

The first comment we almost always get at our workshops in discussing patronage is, "But I don't know any patrons. " Wrong, on two counts. First, given the expanded definition of patronage, you probably know a great many people who can be counted on to assist in your career building efforts. And second, you often don't realize whom you actually know. It's important to identify individuals who do or may support you, and then to understand their motives for doing so.

Patrons are people who have enough time and/or money to be able to spend some of it on you. They may be found among

- Your family;
- Organizations - religious, fraternal or civic;
- Alumni associations;
- Your students/ Parents of students;
- People at your outside jobs.

All of these include people who have some reason to be interested in you already. This is vital, for reasons which will be explained later. To these can be added:

- People you meet through your performing activities.

The people who will ultimately support you and your work are people who a) are able to do so, and b) like and/or admire you. Look for potential friends in potential sponsors. Find something in common. And then, keep these people in your address book, with correct spellings and current phone numbers and addresses. Add to the list regularly.

Knowing your potential individual patrons involves understanding what their philanthropic motives might be. They might include the following, in no particular order:

- Many of today's potential patrons came of age during the '60s. The values they embraced then may have been submerged during the scuffle to make a significant place for themselves in the business or professional world, but will often surface again when they've achieved some success and perhaps had a family. At this point, they may seek ways to reintroduce more spiritual values into their lives.

- They may want to feel important. Being a patron of the arts usually brings with it a special status which can enhance other areas of the patron's life.

- They may be frustrated musicians, individuals who took piano lessons as children and dreamed of performing on the world's great stages, but took the safer route and went into the family business. Assisting someone who is taking the risk and making music her life may be a way of maintaining their direct involvement with something once very close to them.

• They may, surprisingly, be assuaging a certain amount of guilt about their success. Many individuals who have "made it" are aware that a field like music, requiring complete dedication and endless effort, doesn't offer the same financial rewards that their own fields do, and are interested in righting the balance in some way.

• They may simply love music. Helping to make fine music, your music, possible, will be all these individuals want or expect. These are rare people, and to be treasured.

Remember that we're discussing individual philanthropy, and not institutional giving, where money has been set aside specifically for giving away, and the reasons for support are often clearly stated in published guidelines.

Also, needing a tax break has not been included on the list of motives. For one thing, gifts to private individuals are rarely tax deductible, and you therefore would need a non-profit organization to receive tax-deductible contributions for you (see General Resources section). For another, the tax laws do change about what and how much is actually deductible. Nonetheless, this does remain an attractive reason for a contribution for some people.

If people do provide support of any kind, what do they want in return? Simply, they want to be acknowledged, in order to share in the glory and experience the pride which comes from having made something significant happen. When they come backstage after the concert, when you're accepting the congratulations of all, they want to hear some version of "I couldn't have done it without you" from you. The moment of reflected or shared gory is unbelievably exciting, particularly to those whose own lives rarely offer direct applause, but even to those of us who sometimes do perform ourselves. *The degree to which it is exciting, and therefore to which the patrons are motivated to work towards making it happen again, is directly proportional to how well they know, like, and identify with the artist.*

In other words, you need to give away a little, to share the spotlight, in order to get more back. *Whatever you do say, it should be the truth, and should express a sincere awareness that somebody else helped you.* Since no performance is really possible without some kind of support, from the audience or from those behind the scenes, when you say thank you, you should mean it.

Before going into specific advice, it is important to remember that no matter how good the cause for which you're seeking support, how capable the potential patron is of giving it, and how faultlessly a request is presented, you will probably get "no" for an answer. Be prepared for a considerable amount of rejection, and don't take it personally if possible, as there may be endless reasons - none of which may relate directly to you and your project - why someone responds negatively rather than positively. There will be more about dealing with rejected requests later.

How do you start? Specifics of Making Requests

You are probably reasonably comfortable asking people to attend your concerts, at least by mail, particularly if you're willing to provide free tickets. However, asking for anything more can seem an insurmountable problem.

Asking people for support is a kind of sales, which, believe it or not, can be fun, or at least interesting; it can be a challenge to try to convince people to do what you want them to do. If you believe that in fact you're giving them something of value in return for this support - and hopefully the remarks of the previous paragraphs will have demonstrated that philanthropy involves an exchange - you should feel that a successful deal will benefit both parties.

Here are some possible requests, in ascending order of commitments of money or time, and some approaches to getting a positive response.

To come to your concerts

- Don't just send a flyer; write a note on the flyer, asking them to come.

- Keep on writing these notes for every event.

- If at all possible, call or write a note later thanking them for showing up.

To hold a special performance
at the patron's home or business

Perhaps you (or your group) want to do a fund-raiser for a project you have in mind, or need to increase the attendance at your concerts and beef up your mailing list. Perhaps you need to perform in a particularly nice setting for someone important, such as a manager.

Ask advice. Sit down with Joe, who by now has been coming to your performances regularly, and with whom you've struck up a rapport over the years, or sooner if you are particularly kindred spirits (you're both from Texas; you're interested in the relationship of computers and new music technology, and he's a computer specialist; you share a special interest in French music; you share an interest in French food). Tell him your goal (as described above) and your problem (that you need the perfect spot and an audience for a special performance). Let him help you come up with the answer, which might be,

> "Why don't we hold the recital at my apartment? I could serve wine and cheese, invite a group of music lovers, and ask for contributions to [the new recording]."

Or,

> "I don't have room to host a party myself, but I'm a member of a club which holds a concert series; let me make a call or two for you, and we can take it from there."

You might get a completely different response, suggesting an alternative approach to solving your problem:

> "If you want to increase attendance at your performances, perhaps instead of holding a special performance I could offer a block of free tickets to people at the office. I could even take several of them out to dinner first, to make sure they get there; I would

get everyone's names and addresses for your mailing list in exchange for the seats."

You might have to help Joe to advise you, but chances are that given the opportunity he'll be delighted to try to help you come up with what you need. Be persistent, but also be sensitive to when it's time to back off and ask elsewhere. Also know that the responsibility for making an event like this come off is yours. Without being a pain, you will have to keep track of deadlines, remind Joe of what needs to be done, offer much assistance, and write the appropriate thank you note(s).

To provide in-kind contributions

These can be as good as money, and might include such items as free printing of flyers; the donation of a piano from a local company so that you don't have to rent one for a concert; the loan of a tux or gown, or getting someone to buy such an item for you; donated labor, ranging from help with mailings to legal work.

The procedure is the same as above. Ask advice. Be sure that the person you're asking is someone with whom you have a friendly relationship, usually developed over a period of time, someone you have reason to know is interested in you. Make sure that your request is phrased in a way that lets the requested a) give you exactly the response you want, b) propose alternatives, or c) say no, gracefully. Make sure, however, that the request is taken seriously. Write a thank you note, and keep in touch.

All of these examples are descriptions of actual contributions made by real patrons for real musicians we know. None of the musician-recipients are rich or well-connected or famous. And these aren't isolated examples, but typical of exchanges between patron and artist.

Money

This is what most people feel they want from patrons. Think carefully if money is what you really need most, and for exactly what you need it. Generally, requesting the rent and food money (though this may well be your greatest need) isn't going to get you a contribution; rather, a potential patron will probably be more interested in contributing to the costs of a project. Examples of projects which might attract financial sponsorship include:

• Doing the competition circuit, and putting together the funding for travel, accompanist fees and the like.

• Producing a particular concert or making a recording.

• Commissioning a composer.

• Buying a new instrument.

When asking for money, you can ask in person, which means again following the basic **"ask advice"** format above, and developing a strategy together with your advisor. You may prefer to write, however. A personal letter, requesting assistance with funding for travel, for example, might read like this:

Dear Veronica,

Thanks so much for attending my recital last June. It was wonderful to see you there and to visit at the reception afterwards.

As you've been following my career efforts during the past few years, you'll perhaps agree with my teacher and me that the time has come to test my skills against those of my peers around the world, and compete in several European and American competitions. To do so, however, requires funding, for travel costs, accompanists and the like, and there are no scholarships available for this purpose. I've saved $1,500 of the $3,000 I will need to do the Lisbon, Bucharest, and U.S. Interesting Artist of the Year Competitions, and need to find the additional $1,500.

Any contribution you might be able to make would be very much appreciated, as would any suggestions you have about other possible sources of assistance. Please let me know as soon as possible if you have ideas or can help directly, as I must complete entry forms by the end of next month.

Thank you so much for your help and support, both with this project and over the years. Do give my regards to Reggie and the children, and I look forward to hearing from you soon and seeing you at the next recital!

Love,

Archie

Regarding this letter, particularly note the following:

• Archie knows Veronica well, and refers to the fact that she has been following his career over the years. Knowing someone over time is especially important in solicitations for money. You need to have built up credibility and familiarity with you as a person and as an artist. The only exception to this is when a recommendation that you write this letter has been made by another individual that the potential patron knows very well – so it comes to the same thing, they may not know you, but they know your sponsor.

• Archie hasn't indicated a specific figure, since in this case he doesn't want to limit the amount the patron is willing to give, nor to indicate that a given amount is too little. In some instances, you might want to indicate particular figures (a low-high range, for example, or a specific amount being requested from each patron), always keeping the person from whom you're requesting the money in mind.

The amount you request should never come as a shock because it's out of line with the patron's means, the depth of the relationship or the project cost. A board member of Concert Artists Guild, whom we will call Ann Jones, describes having introduced a chamber group of young artists she was sponsoring with in-kind help to a group of friends from her club. It seemed to the artists and to Ann that the club members could be approached for financial assistance; although the artists had just met them, and had performed at the club only once, an interesting project had just come up. After Ann checked with the club members to prepare them and make sure it would be all right, she gave the artists permission to write a letter.

A figure had never been mentioned, and Ann's assumption was that they were seeking a small sum, based on the limited time any of them had known each other. The artists didn't show Ann the letter before it went out. To the club members' astonishment, and to some degree annoyance, the amount the group wanted was $5,000. This was too much to ask, on the basis of a very slight acquaintance. To the patrons' credit, and thanks in no small part to Ann's careful smoothing of ruffled feathers, little permanent harm was done to the developing relationships, though the group didn't get any money.

On the other hand, another CAG board member talks of having received a solicitation for the production of a series of concerts by a young pianist in whom she had developed an ongoing interest over a number of years. The letter limited the suggested donation amount to $100, when she would have been happy to give $1,000.

108

Sample Request Letters

Dear Betty,

It was good to see you at Archie's recital last June, and to visit at the reception afterwards. Clearly we're both devoted fans of his music!

His teacher feels that that the time has come for Archie to test his skills and talent against those of his peers around the world, and compete in several important European and American competitions. To do so, however, requires funding, for travel costs, accompanists and the like, and there seem to be no scholarships available for this purpose. I happen to know that he's saved $1,500 of the $3,000 he'll need to do the Lisbon, Bucharest, and U.S. Interesting Artist of the Year Competitions, but he needs to find the additional $1,500.

I'll be donating several hundred dollars to the "Archie Travel Fund." Any contribution you might be able to make would be very much appreciated, as would any suggestions you have about other possible sources of assistance. Please let me know as soon as possible if you have ideas or can help directly, as Archie must complete entry forms by the end of next month.

Love,

Veronica

If a non-profit organization can legitimately act for you, the donors might well be able to take the contribution as a tax deduction, an added benefit. A chamber group or other musical organization with which you're associated might be incorporated not-for-profit (alternative term, same thing). Other non-profits which might ask for funds on your behalf might include a school, church group, civic organization, or foundation which regularly acts on behalf of individual artists.

The following is a letter Concert Artists Guild wrote to potential donors of funds toward the purchase of a new violin for a young artist. Note that she provided most of the names to which we wrote, though we also sent letters to our own board of directors and membership.

Dear Friend,

From time to time, Concert Artists Guild tries to assist artists on its management roster - winners of the annual International Competition - with special projects. This letter is about one such venture.

Violinist Susan Smith made her Carnegie Hall debut during the 2002-2003 season, as a First Prize Winner of the 2002 Competition. Her extraordinary artistry was lauded by The New York Times in their review, which began, "Susan Smith has the potential to change the way we think of the violin." Her career is moving ahead with impressive speed, and her recent and near future activities include a tour of Italy, performances at the Boston Early Music Festival, appearances with orchestras and in recital around the country, and a New York concerto debut at Alice Tully Hall in the fall.

Ms. Smith badly needs a new violin. She has found one that she loves; it costs $12,000, a reasonable price, but well beyond the means of a young artist. Concert Artists Guild is working with Sue to find funds to purchase the instrument; we felt that some of you would be interested in helping her to do so. Any donation you could give, however small, would be welcome, and would be tax-deductible.

We hope that you do contribute, and extend our thanks for your consideration of this project!

Executive Director
Concert Artists Guild

Guidelines for individual fund-raising

1. Ask advice. It's flattering, and doesn't put you or the patron in an awkward spot.

2. Ask for the specific help that you need. If you're asking for money, don't limit a dollar amount simply through shyness; try for lots, if appropriate, and be informed enough to know when it's not. Be ready with carefully prepared and accurate budgets to back up your request.

3. Expect more rejections than acceptances.

4. Don't phrase requests in a way that will make it uncomfortable to ask the next time.

5. Personalize all requests.

6. Develop patronage relationships gradually! Start small.

7. Don't ask for too much too soon. Assume that in general a patron has to get to know you, and you them, before a request (particularly a large one) is appropriate.

8. Get someone else to write letters on your behalf, if necessary and if you think it will help. Realize that what you may gain, i.e., not feeling awkward, may not be worth what you lose, namely the personal contact which may be vital to the patron.

9. Be careful regarding the details. Nobody will give you anything if you consistently spell her name wrong.

10. Ask for support for specific projects, so that the patron can see the result of his support and be properly acknowledged.

11. Say thank you and keep in touch! Let those you've asked know what happens with the project, even if they haven't contributed, since this may build credibility for the next time.

Conductors

Many of the ideas for this section are drawn from the caring and informative (and very entertaining) talks given at the Career Moves workshops by conductor Murry Sidlin; other speakers on this topic who provided important ideas are conductors JoAnn Falletta, Ransom Wilson and David Gilbert.

It is important to audition for, work with, and get to know conductors for many reasons, not just because it would be nice, if you are a performer, to have the concerto work, and if you are a composer to get the occasional orchestra commission. Conductors talk to lots of other people in the business: managers, presenters, administrators, and performers. They may talk about and recommend you. They also travel a lot and can get your name around. They are considered important people in the field, and their opinions are taken seriously, so that simply being well thought of by conductors can be very valuable in your career building efforts.

There are about 1500 orchestras in this country, designated as community, urban, metropolitan, regional, and major, by the American Symphony Orchestra League, depending on budget size. Almost all of them feature soloists at some time or other. About 20 of them are for all intents and purposes inaccessible to you, the emerging artist These are the most famous orchestras, with the world famous conductors and, generally speaking, the name-brand soloists. Though occasionally unknown artists perform with these orchestras or audition for these conductors, the channels for doing so are carefully and protectively set up: that is, through regular youth competitions, auditions arranged by powerful managers or teachers, and the like. The other 1480 or so, however, are worth a try.

Further, within this large group are those conductors who are your peers, who are of particular interest to you – younger, emerging artists at a career stage similar to your own. The fact that you may already know them as colleagues is a help, and they're probably relatively accessible; not as many performers are vying for their attention, and their schedules aren't yet booked up. If they are gifted and ambitious they will appear in important venues in the future, and will remember you.

In order to get a conductor - or anyone - to pay attention to you, you first have to establish some common ground, an understanding of why knowing each other is in your mutual best interests. Therefore, as with all your other networking, you have to do some in-depth preliminary research (about your customer, the marketplace and what you have to offer) to determine whom to approach and how. Your "customer" at a given time may be the conductor, or may include the particular orchestra where you're contacting her.

Taking conductors first as individuals apart from particular orchestras, you have to know what their musical interests are. What kind of repertoire is he interested in or does he actively champion? Does she seem to enjoy working with young or emerging artists in any of their conducting situations? What kind of musician is he, temperamentally and stylistically? Then, where does she conduct, and what kind of conducting schedule does she maintain?

All the various orchestras they conduct also have artistic profiles as well as budgetary, seasonal, and structural limitations which are important for you to know. What kinds of concerts does the orchestra produce? Does the orchestra's season include run-out concerts, in-school or "kiddie" concerts, special events and non-subscription concerts in addition to their regular subscription season? (These may offer more likely opportunities for unknown artists than the main subscription programs.) Does the orchestra ever hire lesser known solo artists, for any of their programs, under any circumstances?

There are other general limitations which will be useful to know before contacting the orchestra, including whether they have ever programmed soloists other than pianists and violinists, the lead time on planning their seasons, or how much input boards of directors, orchestra committees, or others have over the choice of programs and soloists. (This last is very difficult to find out, and you can't ask directly, but if you happen to come by the information one way or another it is very useful.)

The next thing to clarify in your own mind is what basis you have for contacting the conductor to request an audition. The very best one is that you already know each other, and the conductor knows and likes your music-making; you might have gone to school together, played together in an orchestra or chamber group (performers do move on to conducting, more and more), or you might have played under this conductor at a music festival or as the winner of a competition. Next best (though sometimes even better) is a recommendation from someone known to and respected by the conductor, particularly if this person is willing to make the call on your behalf, and not simply to let you use his or her name. In either of these cases, it would be much more difficult for the conductor to leave your request completely unread and unanswered (though this will certainly happen some of the time).

If you're approaching someone cold, you have to find something which will interest the conductor, to keep your letter out of the circular file. The reason can be either musical or extra-musical; either can work (or fail).

Examples of the latter, extra-musical reasons:

- You come from the town or region in which the orchestra is based. Many orchestras consider it part of their mission to provide opportunities for local musicians.

- You have some past regional or personal association which gives you something in common with the conductor (a relative, your elementary school, having worked at the same non-music job. You get the idea).

Examples of the former:

- You share a repertoire interest (the music of a particular composer or period).

- You can offer a premiere of a work commissioned by and/or for you which would interest the conductor.

- You do special programs (for children, for example) which would be useful for the orchestra's season.

- You've received glowing notices and packed houses in the area for previous solo performances, and are something of a regional favorite.

If you can offer several reasons to read further in your letter, so much the better.

There are actually factors which make an emerging artist at least potentially attractive to an orchestra. These factors include:

Price. You're cheaper than the famous soloists they may hire for many of their main subscription events.

Diversity of musical services. You may be willing to play unusual works, or to learn something quickly when someone is ill, for example.

Special projects. As mentioned above, you might be able to offer the conductor or orchestra something of particular interest - a premiere, or a series of thematically related programs.

Your letter to the conductor must do the following:

- Open with something which will make it likely that it won't be tossed out.

- Follow up with reasons why it would be interesting to hear you.

- Indicate that you're available virtually anytime and anywhere to audition (recognizing how incredibly busy the conductor is) and that, though you are particularly gifted in the musical areas you've highlighted, you're also wonderfully flexible.

- End up by thanking the conductor for his or her time and attention, and attaching well-produced support materials (see Chapter II).

The following page contains an example of a letter (not to be taken too literally, and only in conjunction with the notes):

Dear Maestro Smith,[1]

I'm writing you at the suggestion of my friend [pianist][2] Ivan Bigwig, who recently performed with the Argumentative Chamber Symphony under your direction, and who perhaps has already spoken to you about me[3]. As I've recently had the opportunity to hear you conduct here in AnyCity, and was very excited by the wonderful performance (the tempo of the 3rd movement of the Brahms made it make sense to me for the first time)[4], I decided to write immediately.

As you will see from the enclosed materials, I am a pianist who has studied and performed extensively, both regionally (I come from and am based in AnyCity)[5] and around the country, and have won several important competitions both here and abroad[6]. My repertoire is broad based[7], and includes some unusual works in which I believe we share a special interest. I play a new concerto by the distinguished composer Jane Doe, for example, a work commissioned for me. Knowing of your commitment to the works of American women composers, I particularly wanted to bring it to your attention[8].

I would very much appreciate the opportunity to audition for you at your convenience. I could be available for an audition either here in AnyCity when you are conducting here or at your home base in Chicago[9]. I did notice that you will be conducting in Escapeville next April; as I will be performing in the area then, perhaps it would be most convenient for you if I were to arrange for an audition room in the hall in which you'll be rehearsing at an available time[10].

Thanks so much for your time and attention, and I look forward to hearing from you.

Notes on the above:

1. It rarely hurts to call a conductor Maestro. They usually like it.

2. "Pianist" is in brackets because if you and/or the conductor know Ivan well enough, or if Ivan's famous enough, you don't have to say it directly. You wouldn't have to say "cellist Yo-Yo Ma." This goes for other modifiers, such as "your friend, " or "my mother. " If you both already know the contact person, better not to state the obvious.

3. You're indicating immediately that you're a friend of a friend, or at least a colleague. Chances are that the conductor may not be the first to read the letter, or may not ever get to read it himself, but knowing that there's a personal connection makes it difficult to completely ignore.

4. Stating up front that you actually are familiar with this conductor's work, and admire it, is a good idea if it's true. (If it's not true, it makes it somewhat dubious to be asking her for help anyway.) Conductors are people too, not unswayed by praise or criticism. Be as specific in your remarks as you can.

5. Bring up the local connection early, as in a small city or a less artistically glutted region this may help your chances of being of interest.

6. Similarly, being a competition winner helps establish your bona fides as an artist to be taken seriously and with some experience. Be specific and name the competitions, if they're recognizable.

7. In addition to letting the conductor know about your musical specialties, you're indicating that you can do the standard repertoire.

8. Ideally this is true, and you do share an area of special musical interest. Equally important, you've distinguished yourself from the crowd by showing that you're willing to discover, learn and perform non-standard repertoire.

9. You're making it clear that you're extremely flexible about when and where you audition, which is just about essential if it is ever to come to pass.

10. Here you've really done your homework; but knowing and making an audition proposal based on the conductor's touring schedule is either flattering or intrusive, unfortunately depending on the particular individual and not subject to any rules. Generally it would be better to leave a very specific suggestion like this for a subsequent letter.

Follow-up

It is perfectly reasonable to call the conductor's office (where you sent the letter) to ask if it was received. It is also appropriate to talk a bit to the secretary or other staff who might be screening the letters, and learn about whether the maestro holds regular auditions and where, or whether, auditions are arranged on a more ad hoc basis. Perhaps this conductor never does audition, but prefers to hear artists when they're actually performing somewhere. Knowing this will certainly inform your future calls and correspondence. Take this opportunity to ask if there are additional supporting materials which would be helpful for you to send, to be added to your file. (Most orchestras and/or conductors actually do maintain such files.)

Now comes a long period of waiting, during which you have to be both patient and persistent. Write again after three to six months to see if anything has happened. Use this letter to a) update your activities and b) offer a demo CD, particularly if it's one which you know the conductor will want to hear (the world premiere of the Doe Concerto?). Then, periodically write and update your materials.

The updating should never be done with a form letter of the "Dear Friends" variety, but should be personal; it can be short, though. A call to the office (never call at home, unless the conductor has specifically requested that you do so) could be appropriate every once in a while, to determine if auditioning procedures are still the same. During this time of courtship, keep yourself informed about the conductor's and the orchestra's doings; who are they hiring, for what performance situations, doing what repertoire.

At some point, give up on this person, if absolutely nothing is happening and if in keeping informed about the orchestra's and the conductor's progress you sense that you are not the ideal person for them anyway. This is probably unnecessary advice, since it is unlikely that you'll have enough time to beat dead horses, and will have little enough time to pursue live ones. This counsel will only be needed by the most irritatingly persistent people – who should, in any case, tone it down a bit.

If you get the audition - and yes, it does happen from time to time - be careful to present a balanced selection of repertoire, unless the maestro has requested something specific. Definitely include some of the materials you used as bait to interest this conductor in the first place. It isn't necessary to play only concerto material or sing only oratorio arias. Assume that you will need to provide an accompanist. Every once in a while a conductor will want to play for you, but it's very unlikely. Be aware that there may be time constraints, as in any audition situation, and try to maintain an attitude that one Concert Artists Guild friend calls "humble, yet confident."

After the audition, make sure that you write your thank you note, quickly. And then, keep in touch. It is very possible that the conductor or the orchestra can't use you now; by keeping both informed of your activities and repertoire you're remaining well-positioned to be available should an opportunity arise, as well as keeping your name current in their respective memories.

There's another long shot chance here, which is that if the powers-that-be are familiar enough with you and your work, have heard your CD, or are otherwise confident in your ability, they may simply hire you - audition or no audition. Be prepared.

The theme of this section has really been getting to know the conductors, rather than specifically getting them to engage you as a soloist with the orchestra, even though approaching them with the latter in mind has been the illustration chosen. As stated before, whatever the outcome of an audition, conductors can be immensely valuable musical friends and allies. However, when you are specifically looking for concerto (and other solo) work, keep in mind that the advice offered above can be adapted to others in positions of power in a given orchestra. These include managers, artistic administrators, even members of the boards of directors in some cases. If you know or have some connection to these individuals, certainly consider making them a part of your constituency.

Composers ... from the performer's perspective

The ideas for this section have appeared in talks given at the <u>Career Moves</u> workshops by Frances Richard, Director of the Symphonic and Concert Department at ASCAP and former associate director of Meet the Composer.

This chapter shouldn't really be necessary. In a well-ordered world, contributing to the accumulated body of musical wisdom and participating in its creation through performance would be every performer's goal. In that world, the career-building effect of working on an ongoing basis with living composers and championing their works would be the natural by-product of the performer's regular artistic life. Given that we don't live in a well-ordered or particularly thoughtful world, the practical desirability of doing so has to be stated, in so many words.

The career-building value of working with composers is not frequently discussed. The attitude prevalent in many conservatories and among many private teachers is that learning a couple of contemporary works is a burden to be borne as part of a graduation requirement. For many, musical education is the passing on of received knowledge. Some teachers include the contemporary music of their time, even if that is Rachmaninoff and Debussy, as part of that knowledge, but most ignore the music of our own time as being outside that mandate. This leaves the business of seeking out and learning contemporary works to the students, who approach doing so with some suspicion, fearing that it's all going to be very unappealing and unrewarding. Contemporary music also becomes difficult to fit into an already overcrowded practice day filled with learning the "standard" repertoire. But the result of this is to leave the majority of young musicians at a career disadvantage.

We've already discussed why it is necessary to stand out from the crowd of aspiring musicians in some way, and carve out a special niche for yourself in the musical community. Since, sadly, becoming fluent in new music is something relatively rare, you have an automatic advantage if you are. The skills you need in order to learn and perform new music well - good sight-reading and learning quickly, the ability to count, accuracy of intonation and sometimes the ability to transpose, and more - are valued and appreciated throughout the field.

Yes, it's true that if you're a violinist most presenters want you to play the Mendelssohn concerto, and not the Elliott Carter concerto. However, remember that the competition for the Mendelssohn jobs is incredibly fierce, while those who can play the Carter, when there is a call for it, are scarcer than hen's teeth. Interestingly, there is considerable call for performances of new music, since - remember how you have to know where the money comes from, and how it's allocated? - funding sources, both government and private, feel a strong obligation to support the creative work of our time and the groups or individuals that champion it. For example: an orchestra may support its pops concerts on ticket income, and squeak by in its warhorse programs on a combination of ticket income and donated funds, but can get money over and above subsistence for presenting the works of living, preferably American, composers. And someone (you?) is needed to play them. Add to this the number of festivals that feature new music which take place around the country, as well as the new music groups which regularly present concerts, and you're looking at a fair amount of work.

So, playing new music can get you some work: it can also get you significant attention from the press. This is also discussed in the chapter on the press; here we'll say only that by featuring new works on your concert programs you'll intrigue and interest critics, who may come as a result. You may get the interest and attention of your colleagues and mentors as well. A program performed in New York by a Concert Artists Guild ensemble, Antares, featured a rarely heard Ned Rorem piece and two works written for the ensemble by young composers (see the Press Release sent out in Chapter VII). The group was rewarded by the attendance of a New York Times critic and a wonderful review.

Your effectiveness as a performer of new music can be maximized by seeking out particular composers whose music you very much admire, and becoming a champion of their work. The networking value of working with selected composers and becoming identified with these performances is greatly enhanced, and the chances are greater that you'll get at least some of the calls when their music is programmed and a soloist or chamber musician is needed. (Think particularly of younger, emerging and less well-known composers, whose career stage again is comparable to your own, and not just the new music superstars.) In addition, you and the composer can perform together, with the composer appearing with you at performances of his or her music; adding this feature to the performance can make a special program that much more attractive

The effect of performing new music on the way you perform more standard repertoire can be considerable and profound. The musicians who play both are often the ones who are the most interesting. When dealing with wet ink, understanding that each note written represents a decision to go one musical direction and not another, and that such decisions may not be carved in stone (particularly if a work is written for you, and you have some input during the process), can forever change the way you approach even the most well-known works.

Considering all the reasons for performing new music, you might rather wonder why the question isn't "why not?" rather than "why?" We can only think of two reasons, and both involve money. Commissioning can be expensive (though it's not necessarily so), and performing new works, particularly with a group, can involve extensive and costly rehearsal time. Remember, however, that there may be money available from both public and private sources to underwrite the commissioning and performance of new music even when there's no money for anything else, so these obstacles shouldn't be impossible to overcome.

There is one other possible reason which is sometimes expressed for not playing new music, but it has not been included in our list because it's nonsense. To the thankfully dwindling group of musicians that still can be heard to say, "I don't like new music," please remember that there is no one specific "new music." We live in a time of extraordinarily broad-based musical eclecticism, with something to everyone's taste. It's simply a matter of being musically curious and listening actively to find music you at least like, which everyone should do anyway.

If you decide to commission, which confers the greatest prestige and may offer the opportunity to work with the composer on the creation of the music, the how-tos of commissioning, including suggested fees, contracts and more are laid out in a booklet (Commissioning Music) available from Meet the Composer. Additional guidance may be obtained from two major composer organizations: American Music Center and American Composers Forum. (See Chapter XIII, General Resources, for the addresses and phone numbers).

When you perform new works, remember - or learn, if you never knew - that most composers belong to one of two licensing organizations, ASCAP and BMI, which act for them somewhat as a union does for performers. That is, these organizations protect the composer's interests. A composer is entitled to a fee for the performance of her work under most circumstances, and the fee is paid to the licensing group which sends checks to the composer. The fee is generally modest, and is based on the hall's ticket price structure or other factors. These fees form an important part of a composer's income. It is unfair, and also illegal, to deny a fee to the creator when the work is performed. Make it your business, therefore, to know whether a fee is required, who is assuming the fee (often the hall or radio station will take care of this), and whether you should assume this expense as part of the concert budget. For further information on performance licensing, call ASCAP or BMI directly.

VII. The Press and Public Relations

The ideas expressed in this section were largely drawn from very candid and enlightening talks given by Allen Hughes, former music and dance critic and editor of The New York Times. Additional helpful information was contributed by Anthony Tommasini, of The Boston Globe at the time of his participation in our workshops, and now critic at the New York Times.

The press is an essential element in an artist's career building, though not necessarily, or even principally, through reviews. To most musicians, "press" means "critic," and, since an artist's view of musical criticism generally includes both unrealistic hopes and negative expectations, the best of what is to be gained from the press is lost before it's found.

The press is not actually in the business of providing good reviews with which you can fill out your press kit, or even positive, quotable lines for you to reproduce in your public relations materials. Obviously, reviews aren't useless; nice ones are encouraging (and reproducible), and a body of reviews can give you and your supporters some idea of how you are being perceived by your audiences. But it is important to recognize that any particular review won't give you much beyond one person's opinion about your concert. A good review won't create a career, and a bad one won't stop one.

But since your goals include getting people beyond friends and family to come to your concerts and getting hired for additional performances, you must make yourself known to the public. As one member of the press has often said at our workshops, "First the public knows your name; then the public knows your face; then the public comes to hear you play." **To accomplish your goals it is necessary to get the word out, and the press is often the means by which the word is gotten out.**

The press, of course, includes more than the newspapers, comprising the electronic media as well as the vast array of print publications that, in one way or another, serve the field. However, the daily interaction between the arts community and the local newspapers is perhaps the best place to start. As always, it is important to understand their point of view before considering how to convince them of yours.

Newspapers

Newspapers exist, basically, to report the news. They also determine what for them is news - i.e. what are undeniably items of universal importance, and additionally what are the particular interests and priorities of its staff and readership - and therefore what gets reported. For very many newspapers, the way they determine what is news is by counting heads: how many people will be interested in a given item. By this measure, classical music, except in very special circumstances, isn't news, so the very fact that it is regularly reported on at all -whether by reviewing concerts, announcing coming events, or including feature articles of more general interest - is a matter of conscience, a bow to "culture." In almost all cases, someone famous is news, and therefore coverable, in a way that you are not. This is not an insurmountable obstacle to being featured or reviewed, but important to keep in mind.

Much of classical music coverage does indeed consist of reviews, and in many cases reviews are a specialized kind of news. When an opera production or an orchestral concert which is part of a longer run is reviewed, readers can follow up by attending a subsequent performance (as they could in the case of a movie or a play). Performances by individuals or chamber groups are generally one-time only events; even if a concert is part of a series, the specific repertoire won't be repeated. The reader can't respond to a good review by saying "That sounds great!" and rushing out and buying a ticket. In the short term, what the readers get is an opinion as to whether they missed a good concert or were saved from a dreadful one. What the newspaper tries to provide beyond this by printing reviews of single concerts is a sense of who's doing what, where, and – in the newspaper's view – how well.

For each newspaper in each location, therefore, what's news? what's reviewable? what gets covered? is determined by the relationship between the priorities of those in charge and the perceived interests of the paper's constituency. You will need to read your local newspapers to learn who the music writers and editors are, what are their interests and priorities, and what gets printed.

In New York City only one newspaper, *The New York Times*, somewhat regularly reviews concerts by small groups, or lesser-known artists, or debut recitals. The Times seems to assume that their readership includes enough people who are interested in classical music to keep more critics on staff and to cast their critical and reportorial net more widely, and with greater regularity and predictability, than other papers in town. Though a review of a young artist might appear in another paper, it's far less likely. (It's not all that likely even for *The Times*, given the many variables involved; see Chapter V.) This situation may be slightly - or even greatly - less egregious in cities and towns outside New York.

For *The Times*, the inclusion of new or unusual repertoire in a concert program, perhaps a premiere, will be of significant interest and may increase the chances of a program getting reviewed, for three reasons. First, it seems to be the policy of the paper to pay attention to creative work and composers as well as to performers; second, a review which describes a premiere, say, serves both the composer and the performer and brings more information (news) per inch to the general readership; and third, the reviewers are more interested in attending this program, since they won't have heard that same piece twenty times previously in the same season.

For a newspaper in a small community which doesn't have the saturation of musical events that New York City does, a program featuring quite standard repertoire might be of great interest - depending on who the artist is, the artist's relationship to the community, or the group presenting the concert. Even in a larger city, a featured artist who is from the area might be attractive enough in a more "human interest" way to rate a feature article before the concert as well as a review. When this chapter was originally written, we had just read a review of a performance in Miami by a young pianist represented by CAG; we had presented concerts in that same city on this same series for two years, but this was the first time a Miami paper was willing to review one of them. The concert did take place in the summer, when almost nothing else of musical interest was happening, which helped; but even more important, the pianist was born and raised in Miami. This seems to be true in Boston as well; for the *Globe* the priority, in addition to covering the most high profile events, is Boston based artists.

Your information on the interests and concerns of the press in New York or other major metropolitan areas will probably come from familiarity with the publications as a reader, plus some good detective work. In smaller communities though, the people of the press may be considerably more accessible to you, and you can learn a great deal in a much more direct way. It is possible, when planning a concert appearance in such a city or town (and with the approval of those presenting your event), to research the papers that may write about the event, find out who the music or arts editors are, and call them up. You can tell them that you are excited about coming to the community and would like to know more about its musical life, and you might want to ask advice about some aspect of this or a future performance. You certainly want to indicate that you will provide any information about the event that they might require, and that you would happily be available for an interview if that would be helpful. What you're establishing is a friendly relationship, indicating respect for the press' need for information and role in your career development, and laying the groundwork for mutual interest.

Your successful dealings with the press, then, will be based on **mutuality** – on everyone's getting what they need. In spite of the fact that you may feel that you're fighting for space in a newspaper that's basically uninterested in you, this is only partially true. As long as there's interest in music in the community, and the newspapers have to fill the allotted space with something, it is essential to a paper to have information about the field. **You are helping the journalist and critic by giving them something of interest to cover and keeping them abreast of your activities in the field; they are responding by putting your name before the public.**

If any of the advice below on reaching and working with the press results in your being interviewed by a newspaper reporter, consult the section below on *Radio: Being Interviewed* for guidance.

One additional important word, on the relationship of paid advertising to critical coverage. The mutuality referred to above does not include a quid pro quo of "buy an ad and get reviewed. " This is certainly not the way most publications do business; it is against stated policy for music staff to communicate with advertising sales staff before deciding on who gets covered. Should you decide to pay for an ad, do it for its own publicity value, since that's all that will get you.

The Press Release

Your most basic form of communication with the press will be through the press release, a general, non-personalized communication sent to those on your mailing list who might want your information. The release is generally short, ranging from half a page to three or so pages; for most releases, one to two pages will do the trick. You will send a press release (or one will be sent on your behalf) when you are giving a concert, when you or your group has accomplished something special, or when something worthy of public notice has occurred or will occur. Press releases, sent in plenty of time to be useful (see calendar below) are always

>   **Typed**

>   **Double-spaced** (Our examples aren't, exactly, but that's to save space in this book.)

>   **With wide margins,** so that a reporter or editor can make notes.

They always include

>   **The name and phone number of a press contact** (who may be you) at the top, who can be called if the release is considered of interest and if further information is wanted. The release is typed on letterhead or will have the name, address and phone number of the group typed on it, so that it can be easily identified. There is a standardized format for these things, so that press people - who are, after all, barraged with such material - can quickly and easily read them.

In addition, format conventions include

>   **A release date at the top.** Usually your release will be headed "For Immediate Release," meaning that the paper can print the information upon receiving it. We imagine that there are some special cases where a later release date is specified, perhaps to give the press time to prepare for some kind of news bombshell, but we've never seen one.

>   **The word "more" at the bottom of the page,** if the release goes on to a second, third, or - heaven forbid - fourth page.

>   **Pages numbered at the top** with five repetitions of the page number, i.e., "22222," or "33333." Yes, it's peculiar, but that's the form.

>   **"# # #" marks, or the word "End" at the end of the release.**

The release is written in journalistic style, with the traditional who, what, when and where in the first paragraph, and in the inverted pyramid format of the news story - with the most important information up front and the more general, less important, or background information following. The headline which introduces the release should briefly emphasize the most important fact, or facts, about the event being described.

You may want to have several press releases: one short release to give the specifics of a concert for inclusion in an events calendar; one slightly longer release, including some background information, to send to critics who you hope will review the concert; and one lengthier release with detailed background information for those journalists who might be interested in writing a feature, or who need to be lured into the concert hall with stronger ammunition. Examples of each of these follow. Note the dates on which they were sent, relative to the date of the concert.

Example 1: A release intended for calendar listings *in magazines* (note the long lead-in time), with just the most basic information. An events calendar release for a newspaper would only need to be sent a month or so in advance.

Concert Artists Guild

FOR IMMEDIATE RELEASE
August 6, 2002

Press Contact:
Steven Shaiman: 212-333-5200

CONCERT ARTISTS GUILD PRESENTS
ANTARES

On Tuesday October 22 at 7:30 p.m., the chamber ensemble ANTARES, 2002 First Prize winner in Concert Artists Guild's International Competition, performs at Weil Recital Hall at Carnegie Hall, 57th Street and 7th Avenue in New York City. Tickets are $20; students and senior citizens $10. For further ticket information, please call Concert Artists Guild at (212) 333-5200 x 10.

PROGRAM

Stephan Freund: Dodecaphunphrolic (1997)*	Ned Rorem: Winter Pages (1981)
Igor Stravinsky: Suite from L'Histoire du Soldat	John Mackey: Breakdown Tango (2000)*
Paul Hindemith: Quartet for clarinet, violin, cello, and piano (1938)	

*Written for Antares

#

850 Seventh Avenue, Suite 1205, New York, NY 10019
(212) 333-5200/(212) 977-7149 fax   www.concertartists.org   sshaiman@concertartists.org

Example 2: A more complete release, and the kind you would want to use if you have only one. This can be sent to your entire press list.

Concert Artists Guild

FOR IMMEDIATE RELEASE
September 1, 2002

Press Contact:
Steven Shaiman: 212-333-5200

ANTARES AT WEILL RECITAL HALL
CONCERT OCTOBER 22

First in a series of four concerts featuring winners of the 2002 Competition

The chamber ensemble Antares will open the 2002-2003 Concert Artists Guild Series at Weill Hall at Carnegie Hall on Tuesday, October 22, 2002 at 7:30 p.m. The performance marks the first in a series of four concerts featuring winners of the 2002 Concert Artists Guild International Competition.

Antares will present an exciting program of twentieth-century music featuring a performance of Ned Rorem's seldom-heard *Winter Pages* on the eve of the composer's 80th birthday.

Antares (Vesselin Gellev, violin; Rebecca Patterson, cello; Garrick Zoeter, clarinet; Eric Huebner, piano) was named First Prize Winner of the 2002 Concert Artists Guild International Competition. In addition to the First Prize, the ensemble was also awarded the Victor and Sono Elmaleh Prize, the WQXR Prize, and numerous performance prizes from concert series and festivals around the United States. Formerly known as the Elm City Ensemble, Antares has previously won top honors at four national chamber music competitions as well as a Chamber Music America/ASCAP Award for Adventurous Programming. Upcoming engagements include the La Jolla Chamber Music Society, the Krannert Center for the Performing Arts at the University of Illinois, the Hancher Auditorium at the University of Iowa, and the Brooklyn Friends of Chamber Music. Recent performances include the Kennedy Center in Washington DC, the New Victory Theater in New York City, and a three-part series at the Festival of Arts and Ideas in New Haven, CT, as well as international engagements in Brazil, Canada, and Japan.

(more)

850 Seventh Avenue, Suite 1205, New York, NY 10019
(212) 333-5200/(212) 977-7149 fax   www.concertartists.org   sshaiman@concertartists.org

130

Example 2, continued

Concert Artists Guild
22222

    The concert will begin at 7:30 p.m. at Weil Recital Hall at Carnegie Hall, 57th Street and 7th Avenue in New York City. Tickets are $20; students and senior citizens $10. For further ticket information, please call Concert Artists Guild at (212) 333-5200 x 10.

PROGRAM

Stephan Freund: Dodecaphunphrolic (1997)*	Ned Rorem:	Winter Pages (1981)
Igor Stravinsky: Suite from L'Histoire du Soldat	John Mackey:	Breakdown Tango (2000)*
Paul Hindemith: Quartet for clarinet, violin, cello, and piano (1938)		

*Written for Antares

# # #

Example 3: This is a more detailed release. It's designed to stimulate special interest. Note the emphasis on twentieth-century repertoire.

Concert Artists Guild

FOR IMMEDIATE RELEASE
September 4, 2002

Press Contact:
Steven Shaiman: 212-333-5200

CONCERT ARTISTS GUILD PRESENTS ANTARES
AT NEW YORK CITY'S WEILL RECITAL HALL

First in a series of four concerts featuring winners of the 2002 Competition

On Tuesday, October 22, 2002 at 7: 30 PM, the chamber ensemble Antares will open the 2002-2003 Concert Artists Guild Series at Weill Recital Hall at Carnegie Hall. Antares will perform works of Freund, Stravinsky, Hindemith, and Mackey. In addition, in honor of Ned Rorem on the eve of his 80th birthday celebrations in 2003, Antares will be joined by 2002 CAG Competition First Prize Winner Peter Kolkay, bassoon, for a performance of Ned Rorem's seldom-heard Winter Pages. The performance marks the first in a series of four concerts featuring winners of the 2002 Concert Artists Guild International Competition.

Antares (Vesselin Gellev, violin; Rebecca Patterson, cello; Garrick Zoeter, clarinet; Eric Huebner, piano) was named First Prize Winner of the 2002 Concert Artists Guild International Competition. In addition to the First Prize, the ensemble was also awarded the Victor and Sono Elmaleh Prize, the WQXR Prize, and numerous performance prizes from concert series and festivals around the United States. Formerly known as the Elm City Ensemble, Antares has previously won top honors at four national chamber music competitions as well as a Chamber Music America/ASCAP Award for Adventurous Programming. Upcoming engagements include the La Jolla Chamber Music Society, the Krannert Center for the Performing Arts at the University of Illinois, the Hancher Auditorium at the University of Iowa, and the Brooklyn Friends of Chamber Music. Recent performances include the Kennedy Center in Washington DC, the New Victory Theater in New York City, and a three-part series at the Festival of Arts and Ideas in New Haven, CT, as well as international engagements in Brazil, Canada, and Japan.

(more)

850 Seventh Avenue, Suite 1205, New York, NY 10019
(212) 333-5200/(212) 977-7149 fax   www.concertartists.org   sshaiman@concertartists.org

Example 3, continued

Concert Artists Guild
22222

   Actively involved in commissioning new music, Antares has worked with numerous
composers including Ezra Laderman, Stephan Freund, Kevin Puts, and members of the
Minimum Security Composers Collective. The ensemble's two most recent commissions
are by John Mackey as a collaboration with the Parsons Dance Company at the Joyce
Theater in New York, and by Oliver Schneller through a *Meet the Composer* grant.
Antares recently recorded Ned Rorem's Summer Trio on the Newport Classics label, and
has also recorded works by Ezra Laderman and David Schiff. Antares is the Ensemble in
Residence at Wesleyan University, and has also held a residency at Columbia University
for two years.
   Concert Artists Guild is devoted to the career development of the emerging classical
musician. Since 1951, CAG has developed the careers of over 500 instrumentalists,
singers, and chamber ensembles from around the world. CAG'S programs include the
annual international competition, artist management, commissions, fellowships, and
career development workshops and publications. For more information or for tickets
contact at Concert Artists Guild by phone: (212) 333-5200.

PROGRAM
Stephan Freund: Dodecaphunphrolic (1997)*   Ned Rorem: Winter Pages (1981)
Igor Stravinsky: Suite from L'Histoire du Soldat   John Mackey: Breakdown Tango (2000)*
Paul Hindemith: Quartet for clarinet, violin, cello,
                and piano (1938)

*Written for Antares

                                    ###

              850 Seventh Avenue, Suite 1205, New York, NY 10019
   (212) 333-5200/(212) 977-7149 fax   www.concertartists.org   sshaiman@concertartists.org

---

   In all the above releases, note that the information about hall and tickets
ends the body of the release, and that the program is restated last of all. This
should be done even if you have enclosed the concert flyer along with your press
release (which you should do), as, of course, everything will get separated and
something will get lost.

The Pitch Letter

In some cases you may want to send a pitch letter to a selected critic or reporter, suggesting possible areas of interest and reasons why an event or artist is worth covering. This personalized letter might be attached to a release, sent as a follow-up to a release or sent on its own, as long as all the relevant facts are reiterated in it. An example of a pitch letter:

CONCERT ARTISTS GUILD
850 7th Avenue
New York, NY 10019

September 4, 2002

Mr. Sympathetic Reporter
The New York Times
229 West 43 Street
New York, NY 10036

Dear Mr. Sympathetic Reporter:

Enclosed pleased find a press release on the opening concert of the 2002-2003 Concert Artists Guild series at Weill Recital Hall, where we will present the ensemble known at ANTARES, First Prize Winner of the 2002 Concert Artists Guild International Competition. This concert marks the first of our four concerts spotlighting the winners of the 2002 Competition. I hope that you or a representative of *The New York Times* might be able to attend.

Antares is a truly exceptional ensemble, primarily dedicated to 20th and 21st century music, and is in many ways reminiscent of the last new music group to win the CAG Competition – *eighth blackbird*. As you might remember *The Times* lauded the fine performance of Antares in a review of a 1998 concert as the Elm City Ensemble. The highlight of the ensemble's program is Ned Rorem's *Winter Pages*, which the group performs with guest artist Peter Kolkay, bassoon. Antares has worked extensively with Mr. Rorem, and I know he is looking forward to hearing the work performed at Weill. As I know of your particular fondness of the music of the composer, I wanted to extend a special invitation to you.

If you would like more information on Antares, or to arrange for tickets, please do not hesitate to contact me by phone at 212-333-5200 x 16, by fax at 212-977-7149, or by email at sshaiman@concertartists.org. I look forward to hearing from you.

Thank you very much for your consideration.

Sincerely,

Steven Shaiman
Vice President

In this pitch letter the writer is reminding the recipient of two important facts: one, that the program includes at least one work which should interest her; and two, that she already has some interest in or relationship with the performer. There has to be some kind of hook in a pitch letter which is introduced quickly and which grabs the recipient's interest enough to make sure she reads it to the end, whether she acts on it or not. **Don't forget to double check the spelling of the reporter's name and address.**

Note: It may be worth a try to do your follow-up to a press release on the telephone if you have a particularly ingratiating phone manner. If you don't have a good phone manner, forget it. Even if you do, keep in mind that getting people to return phone calls can be a challenging (and possibly futile) undertaking.

Sending Your Materials

What to send

When you send a press release, you will want to accompany it with a minimum amount of support material, if appropriate. If you have a concert flyer, for example, certainly include that (it probably won't be ready for the three-month-in-advance calendar listing release). Don't, however, send a complete press kit, as most of the material in it - reviews from other papers or repertoire lists, for example -won't be of any interest to the receiver, and it will immediately get tossed out. Send a photograph only if you have good reason to believe that it might be printed. It won't be returned, and most large city papers will request one or send their own photographer if they really want one. (That's why you have a press contact and phone number listed, among other reasons.) If you have a general flyer or an interesting background sheet (perhaps your brief biography), these might be all right to attach.

When to send materials

For music or arts calendar listings, call the paper, magazine or radio station (see below) and find out what their timing requirements are. Some magazines need as much as three months to place you in this section. For general and review purposes, three to six weeks lead time is usually enough notice. Much more than that and you may get lost in the shuffle; less, and you stand little chance of being put on the reviewer's schedule. For more extensive releases and pitch letters, two to three weeks before an event may remind the recipient of the concert, and give her an additional reason to attend.

Tickets

Find out (by calling) the paper's policy on tickets: whether they prefer to have them mailed with the press release, or held at the box office or press table on the night of the program in the name of the publication. In any event, tickets must always be

- Complimentary
- A pair, not a single seat
- On the aisle (or some designated favorite seats, if you or the hall - ask them - know which are the preferred seats of that reviewer or paper).

Don't call the paper to find out if the tickets will be used if your purpose is getting them returned; they won't be. Assume that the dozen or so best seats that you set aside for press use are part of the cost of doing business.

When a critic does show up, please remember the following two additional etiquette items:

Start your concert reasonably on time. Critics are driven crazy by having a long wait for the first note.

Don't plant a friend or relative near the critic to
- try and read over his shoulder what his comments are, or
- listen in on his conversation with a companion, or
- engage him in conversation to find out if he likes what he's hearing.

That this would be very rude and irritating should go without saying, but, astonishingly, people do it. You won't, of course.

The Print Press: Beyond Your Own Daily Papers

In addition to your community's daily and weekly newspapers, large and small, there are many other outlets by which your information can be brought before the public. Other print media, the way they relate to your activities, and their geographic coverage, include:

Weekly or monthly newspapers which are community-based, and which list future events even though they do not review concerts. Local.

Home-town newspapers, even if you no longer live or perform in your home town. They will be interested in you anyway.

Alumni magazines, publications issued by organizations or companies with whom you (or someone close to you) have a relationship, and the like. Special constituency, local to national.

Weekly or monthly magazines which include concert listings of future events, and may include reviews of past events, like *The New Yorker* or *New York Magazine.* Regional/ National.

Special interest magazines, such as *American Record Guide,* which both review concerts and recordings and include feature articles. National.

Special interest magazines, journals, and newsletters, which are primarily "to-the-trade" such as *Keyboard Classics, The Strad, The Tubaists Quarterly,* and which publish articles of interest to their own constituency. National (and sometimes international).

The large national weekly magazines *(Time* and *Newsweek)* are unlikely to be writing about you, but if there's a specific interest angle it may be worth a shot to keep them informed. Similarly, other magazines, monthly and weekly, which do not usually include articles about classical music, might be sold on a particular story if you can find an angle which interests them *(People? Elle? Fortune?).*

The Electronic Media

Radio

An awful lot of people listen to the radio. In most communities there exists a mix of stations: commercial, public and college or university based. Even in these very difficult times for classical music radio, classical music may still be included in someone's programming; there may even be a station which still features classical music only. Since the people that would come to your concerts may well be listening to these stations, getting exposure on the air can be enormously worthwhile, and even more useful than print coverage. Often these opportunities will be related to promoting specific concert performances, whether in your home base or while on the road; sometimes, though, they will simply be occasions for the public to get to know you better.

To get the information to a station, about a particular event and about your own availability, you first have to find out what stations are out there, what programs would be interested in you, and who are the producers of the relevant programs. The producer is generally the person who makes programming decisions, and usually is not the on-air person. Sometimes the producer *is* the on-air person, and sometimes an on-air person does have a say in the programming. To find out who the behind-the-scenes people are, and who is involved in programming, you have to call the station.

Send these folks your press release, and follow up with a phone call to emphasize that you would be delighted to come down to the station to perform, if they have facilities for that, or could come down to be interviewed in connection with your coming concert/record release/national tour/whatever. Ask if they would like a copy of your broadcast quality tape (in advance), so that they could play some of it for their audience.

Being Interviewed

The ideas in the following section were, for the most part, generously provided by Thomas Bartunek, President and General Manager at WQXR-FM, the nation's largest classical music radio station.

If any of the above advice is successful, and you are asked to appear on the radio to publicize your concert (or just to fill an interesting hour or so), you will probably be asked to play something, or provide a playable recording, probably a cd - and to talk. It's not that hard and it can even be fun, but there is a knack to giving a good interview. Unless you are very experienced at this, practice, keeping a few guidelines in mind:

Think about what makes your event terrific, and be prepared to say what that is. Write it down, and think about it. You can't say everything during the course of a short-ish radio interview, but you can say something which may draw a potential audience member into the hall. Think about what might intrigue you, were you the listener. There might be two or three things on your list, but no more than that, Too much information will result in a loss of focus, confusing the listener, and making it harder for you to get your points across. Your interview should sound extemporaneous, but it should actually be very well prepared.

During the interview, give answers that contain the above information, no matter what the questions are. Have you ever noticed how politicians handle the press? They keep coming back to the points that they want the public to hear, whether or not they manage to also answer the questions posed. Listen, note the technique, get disgusted with the state of the world, and then adapt the method for your own use. It can be annoying (or infuriating) in a political interview, but it is actually useful and important in an interview with a performer. In this case, the interviewer is not trying to put you on the spot, but rather is looking for that nugget of excitement that you've prepared to give him. He doesn't know what it is until you tell him.

Be prepared with an anecdote or two that will create a personal note and create a connection with your listeners. A story about how you choose your repertoire, or what it means to you, is usually more engaging than the history of the works and the dates of the composers. Something that reveals your humanity - how the string broke during the last performance and what you did to deal with the emergency, for example - creates more sympathy and engages the listeners more than a list of your credits. Try to also show that you care that the audiences enjoy what you will present. Listeners need to know why they should attend your event, and for that they need to know *why you?* and not *why Brahms?* and, above all, *why me - why should I go?*

Don't be thrown by an interviewer who is less-than-perfect, in one way or another. Some radio interviewers are overly enthusiastic, and may never get to interesting content (what our friend from WQXR calls the "Golly! Gee!" school of interviewing); some are hostile; some are friendly and willing, but not knowledgeable; some are quite knowledgeable, but determined to use your interview as a chance to demonstrate this, and make some points for themselves. If you've prepared properly for the interview, just keep coming back - in the most charming way, of course - to the focal point.

Personalize the interview, in or out of town. Always use the interviewers name at some point during the interview: it keeps the interview personal, and shows that you're interested in them as well. If the interview takes place when you're out of town (perhaps as part of a tour), try to include some reference to something local: the sports event which happened the night before, an election result, a concert which took place recently. Find out this information by leafing through the local paper, or by listening to the local talk radio show for a few minutes. It can be very engaging to listeners to feel that you, the visiting artist, are interested in them.

All of the above advice about being interviewed on the radio can be used equally well for an interview with the print press. In that case, you may have more time to consider what you say as it's happening; on the other hand, you have to be extra careful, since what you say won't pass by quickly, but rather will be in print to be read and re-read. Stick to the basic idea of knowing what your message is, keeping it simple by keeping it to one or two important points, including a personal angle, and being interested in and informed about those that are interviewing you, if possible and appropriate.

Getting Other Radio Publicity Free:
Public Service Announcements

Even radio stations which otherwise have no interest in reporting on or playing classical music may help you to publicize an event. Most stations have mandated time devoted to public service announcements (PSAs), and you can try to get your concert included in their public service calendars by always mailing the station the same calendar type release that you send the print press. Find out who at the station receives such notices, or whether they prefer to receive them addressed to "Calendar Listings Editor," or some such title.

It is remotely possible that some station, sometime, somewhere, will be interested in playing your own produced 10, 20, 30 or 60 second spot (taped, ready for broadcast material) on this basis. If you would find it fun and not a huge effort to produce one, either musical or descriptive, go to it and let them know that it's available. More likely the station will be delighted to sell you airtime to play the above; if you have the budget, this can be excellent advertising. (When written PSAs are submitted, your chances of having them read are also increased if you provide 10, 20 and 30 second versions.) Note that you may not be able to include ticket price information in a PSA, so check on this before getting down to the keyboard. Needless to say, paid advertisements certainly can include this information.

Television

As we all know, most people watch television, and most people's view of what's important in the world is formed by what they see on it. Chances are that network television will not be much interested in you. If *Tonight* or *60 Minutes* does call, it will probably be at a stage in your career when you have a public relations representative, and you can oversee his efforts on your behalf instead of implementing the work on your own.

However, with the advent of cable television, the increase in regionally based public television and the enormous expansion in the number of community access and campus stations, opportunities for making yourself better known in a community or publicizing a particular event through this medium are indeed. available. Once you've determined what stations feature community programs or special programs which might be interested in what you do, call and find out who the producers are and add them to your press list. You can then use your calendar listing releases, your general press releases and particularly pitch letters to interest them in featuring you on a program, inviting you on a talk show, or simply including your concert in a community bulletin board listing. Follow all the above procedures about radio as well as the general guidelines for press releases when sending them information. If you have a promotional video of the required length, it also won't hurt to let producers know that you could effectively fill some airtime for them.

WARNING
How about using a Press Agent?

Everything written about (and below) refers to *you*, working on your own behalf. With rare exceptions, artists at the early, or even middle stages of their careers don't need the services of a professional press representative or public relations person or agency. There simply isn't enough there for them to sell. Without goods to sell, it's ridiculous to hire an expensive sales person. You can open most of the doors that you need to open at this level yourself; at the point that someone with more savvy, ability and clout is needed, you'll almost certainly know it. Obviously, when you need help with a project, or some additional expertise in a specific area, get it.

Press Lists

Before you re-invent the wheel, find out who already has a good press list that you can use to get started, or, preferably, several lists that you can combine. If you can't get access to a press list, you can go to the library (head for *Bacon's Magazine and Newspaper Directory* for this information) and the local newsstand, and buy and read an assortment of publications. Spend some time listening to the radio and watching television. (You should do all of this anyway, because you should - to belabor the point yet again - know your customer.) But it's never sensible to spend lots of research time when someone has done it for you. Your school or other organization may be a good source for getting a press list, or an orchestra or other ensemble that you're associated with. Mailing lists are often fiercely protected, but press lists less so than, for example, subscription lists which represent cash to their compilers. Ask around, and, if worse comes to worst, do the legwork yourself.

Questions to ask when starting a list or updating one:

(Some of this has been referred to above, but it's handy to have a list of questions to ask when confronted with an actual person from an actual publication on the other end of the line.) Information, obvious and not-so-obvious, that you should have, includes:

Who is in charge of music reporting and reviews? This may be a complicated question. You may have to address your releases to the Cultural Affairs Editor, the Community Affairs Editor, the Community or Events Bulletin Board, the Music Editor or Music Desk, the Features Editor, or any of dozens of other departments and individuals who may have gotten the job of dealing with classical music. (Remember: You should be sending information to editors as well as to the writers whose by-lines you see in the paper, as the editors make assignments. Again, ask how things should be done.) Be open-minded and creative in getting the operator or department secretaries to give you the names and titles of everyone interested in the field. An important word: Be especially nice to the secretaries or other middle people, as they frequently are the only people you will actually speak to, and who therefore hold your press life in their hands. (This presumes that you're lucky enough to speak to a human; voice mail is tougher, though you can try not-responding to the requests to hit various buttons, and waiting for an operator to direct you to a person.)

When you've identified the correct people, get ...

- the correct spelling of their names and their exact titles

- the address to which you should direct your communications, including email addresses if appropriate

- their policy about sending or holding comp tickets at the gate for events

- their preferred lead time for receiving information for various purposes

Even starting with a ready-made list, count on an initial investment of several hours on the phone to check all the information. What will make your list better than those you've been given is that it will be up-to-date, will use everyone's correct and most recent title, and will be correctly spelled. Please don't underestimate the importance of this It takes an extraordinarily broad-minded and understanding reporter to write an article about you when you've chronically spelled her name wrong, or addressed her as "Mr."

Astonishingly few people or organizations update their mailing lists with any regularity. Though correct information will probably not win you points, incorrect information will evoke such negative responses that you should try, at all costs, to avoid it. The easiest way is to have your mailing lists, all of them, on computer. You can, of course, keep up your lists by hand, but it really is much easier to simply format the computerized list for labels or envelopes, note changes as they reach you, and make a series of calls every six months or on an annual basis to check for overall accuracy.

Email

You should be developing a good email list, including all of your regular contacts (fans, presenters, anyone who has an interest in your music) and potential ones as well. This is an excellent way, even without a website (or as a supplement to one) to let everyone know the latest news: an upcoming concert, a personnel change in the group, a grant received. You get the idea.

The Public Relations Campaign

All of the techniques we've described for communicating with the press, and all of the care you've put into creating interesting and impressive materials, are part of an overall public relations campaign. It might astonish you to know that if you do any of the above, you've embarked on a public relations campaign on your own, or your group's, behalf. This may horrify you, but breathe deeply and consider.

One public relations consultant who has frequently spoken at our workshops says that though business people distrust public relations, and certainly are unable to say what it is, they're sure that they need it; whereas musicians, equally hostile and mystified, are sure that they don't. In the largest sense public relations is simply making sure that those in the public eye, or those with extensive public contact (you?), make the most positive use of all opportunities so that they'll be able to stay in the public eye or have more public contact. Everything that you do in regard to getting yourself and your events known should be informed by this understanding. And, given that you understand this, consciously taking charge of your public relations efforts should become somewhat less off-putting.

The public relations campaign consists of all the activities you do and the materials you create in order to promote your artistic ventures, and to make you better and positively known to all your customers. Principles which guide most effective campaigns are logical and simple (though the techniques involved can be very complex, which is why there are specialists in the field). The five which follow are particularly important for you to remember:

> **Your message about yourself should be truthful, clear, and limited to a few important points at a time.** Though at an actual concert the audience may be receiving a message of great complexity and depth, when they get the flyer, or press release, or telephone call announcing it they should get a powerful message of great simplicity and clarity.

> **As much as possible, the same important points should be featured in all of your messages and materials**, so that your customers are reminded of your strengths with consistency. In other words, it is helpful to coordinate the various aspects of your campaign.

Remember that effective public relations requires persistence.
Though you may go through long periods of feeling ignored, keep
plugging away - politely and pleasantly, and with an understanding of
when frequent is too frequent. Positive impressions and recognition are
being created, even when no immediate results seem to be forthcoming.

Effective public relations also requires creativity. If your audiences
are too small, and seem not to include the people you're sure would like
to hear you, find out what vehicles you could possibly use to get your
information to them, and think about what aspect of what you do could
be emphasized to bring them in. If the traditional music press is simply
not going to give you much coverage, perhaps some aspect of your work
would attract the interest of nontraditional branches of the press.

**Last: If you're really not at all good at one aspect or other of the
public relations tasks described in this chapter or in Chapter II -
writing, phone, coming up with unconventional and new ideas,
producing or assessing the quality of your designed materials - get
someone else who's more gifted in these areas to help, or to do them
for you.**

VIII. Management & Self-Management

All management is really self-management. No matter how far you advance in your career, the responsibility for making sure that you keep working, in the way you want to, remains with you. No manager can magically create a career for someone, though it may seem so sometimes.

We've divided this chapter's information into two parts; first we'll deal with the technical details of how professional management works on your behalf, and then with how to manage these aspects of your career on your own.

Management

Many of the thoughts about management, and much of the technical detail about how major managements operate, were provided by two regular speakers at the Career Moves *workshops: Thomas F. Parker, now President of Parker Artists and previously vice-president with Shaw Concerts; and Charlotte Schroeder of Colbert Artists Management. Information was provided also by Robert Besen, formerly CAG's own artist manager and now President of BesenArts, who performed all the services of a major commercial manager, without the 20%.*

In the classical music field, managers perform a variety of services for their clients. They act as booking agents, finding and negotiating engagements. They "service" the contracts they negotiate, which involves making travel and other arrangements and working out production details with the sponsor. They represent their clients in the marketplace - at trade shows for example - keeping their clients' names and activities current with the customers. They may act in a sort of secretarial capacity, keeping track of their clients' various commitments. They will almost certainly arrange for the design and production of the artists' public relations materials, and will, to a limited degree, do public relations work for them. A good management will assume the responsibility for overseeing an artist's entire career development, making sure that engagements are paced appropriately, that the right level of work is being sought and accepted, and that the artist isn't doing things that will damage him artistically in the long run.

But it is for the first of these - getting work and negotiating the fees - that most performers not yet under management desperately want to be. They feel that with a manager they would have as much work as they could handle, and could forget about all the "business" and concentrate on practicing; performers not under management are convinced that if only they were, their career problems would be over.

There is a small amount of truth in this view of management, though not so much in the area of getting a reprieve from non-musical career efforts. The manager's assuming responsibility for dealing with the physical details of a concert engagement does relieve the artist of a certain amount of work, but you'll still have to write your thank you notes, work the room at the reception to make sure that you get re-engaged, etc. More important, though, a good manager can sometimes do two very important things you can't do for yourself:

> 1. There are doors that will be closed to you, acting on your own behalf, that a very well-connected management may be able to open for you;

> 2. Having a manager enables you to say "Please speak to my manager, " at times when that may be absolutely essential to a negotiation. There are some customers out there who simply don't understand that an artist can be absolutely first class and not have a manager. Not as many as you would think, but some.

To begin our discussion, we'll deal with the kind of major international management that, in the United States, tends to be located in New York City around 57th Street (obviously there are lots of geographical exceptions). Many of their clients are more-or-less famous. These firms are probably the ones you think of first, and theirs are the rosters that many of you hope to join. These are useful to use as models, not only because they present the most daunting challenge to those artists aspiring to sign with them, but also because the way they do business holds true for many smaller firms as well.

What are managers looking for?

Commercial artist managements are in business for two reasons: first, because whoever started the business thinks that it's more interesting and rewarding to work with performers than to make widgets; and second, to make some money (the money coming from commissions on artists' fees). In order for the second of these to proceed from the first, the management needs to have artists on their rosters who 1) interest them artistically, and 2) have the potential to earn significant fees. A handful of artists can make money for pretty much anyone who represents them, since the world comes to them. Everyone else - and you would probably be in this category - needs a significant sales effort in order to get to that point.

How do I know that I'm ready for management?

The usual answer to the question of when are you ready for management is, "when you have something to manage." Though somewhat flippant, that's not a bad answer. You need to have at least the beginnings of a career: to have developed some connections with conductors, presenters or other influential types; won some competition(s); or otherwise gotten into the spotlight in order to make it likely that you'll get some engagements fairly soon (thereby financially justifying your place on the roster). In addition, both you and the manager have to know how you fit into the existing roster: how you complement the current list or who your in-house competition will be.

Are there exceptions to this rule, and does anyone ever get onto a major management's roster without this kind of package? Obviously yes, since managers are people, with interests and enthusiasms (and obligations and relatives) like anyone else. If you're a complete unknown, have never made more than $100 per engagement, but have somehow gotten yourself onto such a roster, your job becomes staying on it.

How do I get a manager?

Most performers will not, in fact, get a place on the roster of a major management (those with the great connections, that can open the important doors). That's simply a fact, resulting from the laws of supply and demand. There are a great many of you, and, relatively speaking, not very many opportunities for work, and therefore not a lot of room on the rosters of the middlemen and women (the managers) who make their livings from putting you and the opportunities together.

But some of you will. Even the most prestigious and powerful managements do take on new clients, and some of the largest do so all the time. Their decision to take someone on is based on a number of specific factors (referred to in general above), and may include any or all of the following:

• A very strong recommendation from someone - or more likely many people - whom they trust; that could be another artist on their roster. For example, the recommendation of one pianist by another on a given roster is taken very seriously, since it means that he's willing - if it comes to that - to share a limited amount of work. Conductors' recommendations, whether they're on that particular roster or another, also carry a great deal of weight, as conductors opinions are respected, and their position in the field means possible engagements for a soloist in the future. Recommendations from other very well known musicians, or important individuals in the business, can be equally important. Another manager might even recommend a gifted artist, whom they are unable to take for one reason or another, to a colleague.

• An important career achievement, such as the winning of a major competition, can result in management offers. A manager may feel that even if she is interested in a particular artist, there must be some initial push to help launch a major career, and she may look for the moment when you've gotten everyone's attention as the right one to start further promotion and career building efforts.

• A good fit between the management and the artist. Each management has a style, emerging from the kinds of artists they select to work with, the personalities of those in charge, and the way in which they do business. The management will usually look for artists with whom they expect to work most effectively.

• Who is on their roster at a given time, and who (and what) they think they can sell. A management may have excellent connections in the opera world, for example, but might be hesitant to take on a clarinetist, even one they admire and like, if they have few or no contacts among recital presenters and are not comfortable or familiar with the clarinet repertoire. However if the management has lots of singers already, and doesn't specialize in voice, they may be more interested in working with a clarinetist than in trying to find work for yet another soprano.

• Their own opinions and preferences. Managers do hear artists perform all the time. They are often trained musicians themselves, and even those who aren't quickly develop very strong feelings about artists they want to represent and those they don't. As they should: no one, no matter how gifted, should have to sell something he doesn't believe in.

> **To sum up, you will probably need to have three things to obtain management, *after* you've gotten interest through some strong personal recommendations:**
>
> • The probability that you can get work
>
> • An artist-manager compatibility that makes sales possible
>
> • Enough of a name or reputation, or the potential to develop one quickly, to command a minimum fee of which 20% would be a respectable sum. On a gross fee of $4,000 a manager would generally make $800; the minimum asking fee would probably have to be around that, with the potential to command much more.

Which management is right for me?

Most *major* management firms are looking for artists who have both the potential for and the interest in an extensive international career. Believe it or not, not everyone - and you may be one of these - wants what this entails. It means being on the road much of each year, having little or no traditional family or home life, having only a very limited amount of private time, constant pressure, and more. Some people thrive on this, others hate it. The management will decide whether they think you have the artistic potential; you have to decide whether you have the all consuming desire to have the career which makes the sacrifices worthwhile. If not, there are good management firms which work with artists regionally, and these might be ideal for you. You can get an idea of which firms do what from looking at rosters in the *Musical America International Directory of the Performing Arts,* and knowing or learning something about the career activities of the artists on specific rosters.

Such research is also helpful in figuring out which company [needs] [wants] [might be interested in] you. Above, we've briefly discussed this from the manager's point of view: now, once again from yours. Since some managements clearly work only with singers, don't bother to approach them if you play the cello. In looking over a roster, you may notice that a given management has a very diverse roster but doesn't list a cellist; that could be because the management doesn't want one, but it's just as likely that it's because they're between cellists, and might look at you more seriously as a result.

Each management has its own personality and way of doing business. Some of the major management firms have enormous rosters, and the amount of direct contact you have with the person representing you may be limited. Some of them are smaller, however, and there may be more personal attention. There may or may not be a direct relationship between the amount of personal contact and the amount of work you get, by the way, so to some extent your decision about which kind of management you prefer has to do only with where you're most comfortable.

Once you've made a short list of which managements might be of interest to you, and might be interested in you, it's time to figure out who you know that might recommend you to them, as described above. Don't bother to write cold (without an introduction) to a management, even if you have reason to believe that you'd be perfect for them. It's a waste of time, materials and postage. At lunch one day a highly respected manager from a very major firm said to us, "If [in the letter] they address me as Mr. Smith, and not as Joe, I don't bother to read any further." In other words, if he was being approached by an artist who didn't already know him on a first name basis, he simply wasn't interested. This is an extreme, but the principle -that the manager already knows about you and has indicated some interest even before you approach him - is valid.

Should a letter approach be indicated (if, for example, your conductor friend has said that a particular manager is expecting a letter from you on the basis of a recent conversation), write a simple, friendly letter which refers to the recommendation right up front, and include some relevant press materials. Don't put in too many things; less is more, as always. Include a bio, a picture (if you have a flyer, that's better than a photo) and reviews. Most important, invite the manager to a concert if you are performing in the area in the near future. Managers will travel reasonable distances to hear someone they're interested in, so send a list of coming engagements; if it's long enough, it makes a good impression about your level of activity too. If you have no performances that the manager would be able to get to, offer to send a CD or arrange an audition at the manager's convenience.

If you don't hear anything after a few weeks, you certainly can make a follow-up call, particularly if given permission to do so by your mutual friend. Follow up with this manager periodically, always with the same friendly tone (it doesn't pay to get resentful, even if you feel that your best years are passing by), letting him know about your current activities. When this level of interaction is reached (what Robert Besen calls a holding pattern), very infrequent calls when. something special comes up, mixed with more regular cards, notes, concert flyers and reviews, is a good approach. It may take years to get him to notice you, so don't give up, but don't be intrusive or irritating.

If all the factors listed which would cause managers to be interested in you are in place, they may approach you. You'll almost certainly be approached by someone if you've done something particularly splashy, like winning a first prize in one of the major international competitions, or rescuing a child from a well while not missing a note of the *Symphonie Espanole*. If you do find yourself with the possibility of management, let's consider whether you can afford it.

How much does management cost?

Generally, managers take 20 % of the gross fee negotiated for an engagement as their commission fee. (The standard commission fee for conductors is 15%; for singers in the case of opera engagements, 10%.) This means: if a manager has gotten you a fee of $3,500 for a recital performance in Toledo, they will take $700 off the top. Out of the remaining $2,800 you will have to pay your air fare to Toledo, your lodging (unless someone there is putting you up), your meals (same exception), your accompanist's fee and her expenses, an airline seat for your cello if necessary, not to mention having the gown or tuxedo pressed and hiring the cat sitter. (Typically, this will leave you with $750-$1250 as your net fee.) Using a net average fee of $1000 per engagement as an example, if you play 40 concerts a year you'll net, that is get to keep, $40,000 annually (on a gross of perhaps $120-140,000); hardly a princely salary, but not totally embarrassing by most musicians' standards. At this level of activity and fee, you might well be the envy of many of your colleagues, and you will be considered very lucky to be able to maintain it. We know that you've not chosen to go into this field for the money anyway, but a few numbers to confirm this are sometimes helpful.

This may suddenly make what seemed like an awfully good fee seem far less wonderful. However, you and the manager will (or should) have worked out a level of fee which builds in the commission and expenses and still leaves you with the net fee you've decided you can accept after all is paid. Also, tax laws change, but as of now all expenses - including commissions - are tax deductible.

The 57th Street managements and their peers elsewhere will generally limit their fees to commissions and not take a retainer (more on retainers later). They're able to do this since the more established artists on their rosters bring in enough commission money to pay the rent and everyone's salaries, thereby floating the cost of getting you established (a period estimated by at least one of our expert consultants as 5-10 years) for at least a while. Until your commissions start rolling in, the firm will cover the costs of staff time and overhead.

What they can't cover are the direct costs related to the handling of your account. Your management will probably do the following, all of which you will pay for:

- Have flyers designed and printed; possibly require new photos, and certainly have photos printed

- Do mailings on your behalf (photocopying, labor and postage)

- Place advertisements (your part of an overall ad for the management, say in the *Musical America International Directory of the Performing Arts,* will be pro-rated)

- Produce, make copies of and distribute demo CDs, videos and other such materials

Other items which, depending on the management firm, you will often have to pay for:

- Phone calls made on your behalf. You'll be billed either for all telephone charges made while servicing your contract, or these plus a pro-rated amount of the general phone bill, or according to some other formula.

- Travel and expenses related to attending sales conventions. Some firms may not charge you for this, but others will pro-rate an amount which will appear in your billing statement.

All of these costs will be charged to you as monthly (or other periodic) bills, or will sometimes be deducted from fees before they reach you. In any case, an itemized statement will accompany your bill, or should.

Some real numbers

Here are some average start-up costs for a young artist newly on the roster of a major management:

Photographs $1,750
Many young artists newly on a big management roster (a competition winner, for example) will either not have good photographs, or will need more up-to-date ones. Probably would need to include color, as would the flyer cost listed below.

Flyers $3,500
This is for a run of about 25,000; presenters at this level usually expect to be provided with 500 – 1,000 flyers at no cost to them, so the management wants to be prepared for 25 to 50 such engagements.

Mailings $1,000
Though the management may well absorb many of these costs if part of their general mailings, this item reflects a typical one-time piece - say, to announce the artist's new management affiliation. We're assuming one such mailing in the year.

Ads $500
This represents a pro-rated amount of major ads in the Musical America annual and the Symphony Magazine annual, divided among 50 artists.

Demo CD duplication $300
We've assumed that the cost per CD with budget envelopes would run about $1.50 - $2.00.

Since these items may vary we've not totaled them up. However, it's clear that an initial outlay of over $7,000, often without much income coming in that year to offset it, wouldn't be very unusual.

What am I responsible for ...
and what is the management responsible for?

Remember what was said above about what you will be bringing to a management in the first place? You will have already developed a list of possible jobs on your own, which, depending on the stage things have gotten to, need to be seriously pursued or only to have the arrangements completed by your manager. In the course of your work, you'll develop more such contacts, and refer them to your manager to pursue, negotiate or complete. In these cases you'll have made the original contact. And in these cases, the manager will almost always take the standard 20 % commission, leading to the main complaint we all hear about managers:

"I get the work, and all she does is take her 20%!"

Let's lay that one to rest immediately. For the first couple of years on anyone's roster, the manager usually will rely on you to provide work opportunities, since it takes her that long to make contacts for you, build up some credibility, and book you several seasons down the line (most engagements are contracted six to eighteen months in advance). The artists who complain the loudest about this problem are often the ones who change managers every two years, thereby almost insuring that their complaints will continue to be justified forever. Next, the 20% is only partially a "finder's fee"; it also goes toward the servicing of the contract, which is a lot of work. From the manager's point of view, the commissions she gets on artist-referred engagements, which are relatively easy money, help amortize the expenses incurred trying to produce engagements that don't come through.

In addition, many good managers in this area of the business (that is, classical music) do not see themselves primarily as booking agents. Though your manager should in the long run be getting you work, and increasingly good work at that, at the start (and much of the time thereafter) she will use your contacts as a starting place for negotiating higher fees than you could get on your own and providing follow-up by servicing the contracts in a highly professional manner.

You have to have a talk with the manager to find out what her contacts are like, in addition to how much she expects from you, and how much and what level of work you can reasonably expect after a few years. In other words, in the area of getting the jobs, you have to assume much of the responsibility, and with some managers - even very fine ones - you may have to assume almost all of it. Further information about where these jobs come from in the first place is in the self-management section.

It is the manager's responsibility to find out everything about a concert that will help you to make it a success, and to let you know this information as clearly as he can. The management will be making travel arrangements, finding out whether there are opportunities for publicity through radio broadcasts or press interviews (and checking your availability for these), investigating whether a performance could be paired with a master class to make you a little more money (if you want to do these), and whether there will be a reception at which everyone will be offended if you don't attend. You may have to prod a little to make sure all these bases are covered. Sometimes he will provide even more information and assistance, like finding out whether there's anyplace to eat at midnight, or how you can get back to the airport if the sponsor's ride falls through.

Though your manager will arrange for you to have sufficient promotional materials, and will probably want to make them consistent with the materials of other artists on the roster, these materials do represent you to the world; you should know what's being used and whether you think there's room for improvement. In addition, you are responsible for keeping an ongoing dialogue going with your manager. She should certainly call you when she's trying to set up an engagement; but you may call her when you want a press release sent out on your behalf (that you will pay for) -say, when you're doing the premiere of a commissioned work that you know will evoke some interest. You'll want to call her to discuss programming, both overall and for particular performances; you'll probably be calling each other if you win a competition. So, the responsibility for the public relations and internal communications aspects of your career is a joint one, though primarily yours.

Alternatives to major management

Medium Size and Smaller Management Firms
Personal Representatives

A brief glance at Musical America will convince you that the world doesn't lack managers. There are hoards of them. Though many of them are in the mid-size range, we will pass right on to discussing small managements; for the medium size companies, you should average out the remarks about major managements and those about small firms. That is, not quite as much power as CAMI (Columbia Artists Management) or ICM (International Concert Management), but more than a small firm just starting out, and so on.

Needless to say, few of the small firms out there have the clout which enables them to pick up the phone and get, say, an audition with a famous conductor for a young artist. When you join the roster of a smaller firm without these major contacts, however, you may be trading off clout for hard work on your behalf, since you might represent a more significant part of their action.

If you are offered a place on such a roster, certainly check the firm out before signing on the dotted line. They should have *some* contacts. Even a young manager just starting out should have developed a few relationships, through previous jobs or other circumstances, which could yield performance opportunities for you. Speak with others on the roster, with presenters who might have worked with them or their artists, or with anyone else who might be acquainted with the firm's operations and reputation. Organizations like ISPA (International Society of Performing Arts), APAP (Association of Performing Arts Presenters) and NAPAMA (National Association of Performing Arts Managers and Agents) act to some degree like Better Business Bureaus for managements. That is, they define a code of ethical business practices for their members, though they don't check up on them as far as we know. Membership in these may indicate a certain level of substance and of participation in the musical community. However, it is still particularly important for you to be assured, through personal recommendations and experience, that the people with whom you are entrusting much of your professional life are going to treat it with honesty, care and ability.

Generally, even a small management firm will operate according to the general financial arrangement outlined above. However, since they may not have the built-in bankroll that established artists represent, some may ask for a monthly retainer to keep them in business while they, as well as you, are getting established. We used to advise artists to stay away from retainers, and still advise against them in the case of large, major firms. However, the realities of the field have changed enough to justify such retainers in the case of smaller firms and those just starting up. You'll have to be absolutely convinced that the manager will be working hard on your behalf, and will take on even more responsibility for keeping in touch and up to date than usual, in order to justify this arrangement. Investigate the firm thoroughly before accepting such an arrangement, and try to move to a commission basis as soon as possible. In addition to retainers and commissions, you will still be paying all expenses, so this can amount to a lot of money. (Retainers are often in the $300 to $400 a month range.)

An artist's representative may be your manager at a small management firm with a staff of one, or he may be an unaffiliated person you specifically hire to perform any or all of the services listed in the beginning of this section. The person you select may therefore be your secretary or assistant, in effect, helping you develop press materials and sending out press kits on your behalf, keeping your calendar, making sure your mailing list is up to date, dubbing tapes, etc. This person would be paid for such secretarial work by the hour or as a weekly or monthly salary. If he has an interest in and talent for sales and booking, by all means train him to assume these responsibilities too - assuming that he's better at sales than you would be. When he starts to work on getting you performance jobs, he can be paid both by the hour and by commission; if he's doing well at booking, you can move to paying on a strictly commission basis. For more about this, see the end of the next section, "Self Management."

Artist-run Group Managements

A group of musicians can get together and hire a personal representative (on a commission basis, preferably, but possibly on retainer) to act on behalf of all of them, thereby starting up a small management themselves. Another alternative to commercial management is an arrangement whereby like-minded performers get together and assume administrative and financial responsibility for management activities for members of the group. Both these possibilities can have several advantages over individual self-management: they can enable group members to pool information and contacts, to spread the work and cost of self-management among the members or allocate it to a salaried person, allow the member musicians to control the kinds of musicians on the roster and allow the members to say, "Call my manager," with honesty and confidence.

A group management can be set up according to the preferences and abilities of the members. If there is one individual who is particularly good on the phone, that person can do much of the telephone booking work; if someone is good at graphic arts, he can assume responsibility for designing the graphics. Someone with a good business sense should take care of the bookkeeping and financial management, and those with no particular skills (other than playing) can certainly pitch in to do mailings and other time consuming tasks. Almost certainly one energetic individual will actually end up doing most of the work; but there should be an agreed upon structure in place, formally, so that this poor person can complain when necessary. The group can decide what everyone's performance fees should be, and how much of a percentage should be charged over and above that to run the management. Be sure to work all this out before starting, to avoid conflict later. You'll be starting a business, and this is always expensive. Therefore, do it intelligently, and with as much advance planning and good advice from those who have tried as possible.

It is always possible, in the best of all possible worlds, that the person inevitably saddled with most of the work will a) like it, and b) realize how much money in commissions is going into the general pot which could be providing her with a living. At that point, she will turn into the manager, and the self-managed group will have turned into a group of artists with a commercial manager. In the one case we know in which an artist started a management on behalf of his own and a few other groups, general expenses were shared among the member groups and almost all of the clerical work was contracted out. The artist-turned-manager himself worked only on commission, which was 10 % rather than the standard commercial 20 % . He enjoyed the excitement of the work and the contacts he made, and was willing to work for no retainer - in other words for almost nothing at first - until the firm started moving. He was very successful, by the way, and the firm - now in business for about eight years - is now operating on a standard commercial basis.

For any of the above models, check with local officials to determine what you have to do to start a management business, if you plan to use the management to actually do anything for you beyond picking up the phone. You will need to legally be a business in order to receive and write checks and the like; acquiring a federal employer's identification number and filing a self-proprietorship is not actually that hard to do, and won't take much of your time.

Self-Management

Many of the ideas and methods set forth in this part of the chapter, and some of the actual words, were conceived by William Matthews, a gifted classical guitarist with more than usual skill (and success) in self-management. Another rare musician who shared ideas, information and insight with us was Laura Spitzer, a remarkable pianist who has toured throughout the U.S., often towing her own piano with her to underserved, rural venues. Laura's remarks will be specifically cited below. The "20 second introduction" exercise is the brainchild of Jedediah Wheeler, one of the more creative and innovative people in the business.

At the beginning of this chapter, we stated that all management is really self management. For most musicians, having a manager doesn't solve the problem of getting work, and you will still be handling much of this responsibility yourself. All the rest - producing materials, determining travel and other schedules, and all the endless detail of making a performance happen - simply means an investment of time of which most artists could and would like to make other use.

Also, for many musicians with management but not with the large and prestigious firms, the economics of the situation seem to make no sense. It's quite possible, after paying the costs of printing a new flyer, the monthly charges for mail and phone, and possibly a retainer fee, that there's little or no profit left for you out of the fees on the few dates you'll get. If this situation is still true after a number of years, with your career stabilized at a limited number of engagements each season, self-management seems a logical and possibly better alternative.

But there are two immediate problems in grappling with the concept of being self-managed. The first has to do with self-image; usually, artists can't help but feel - albeit deep down - as the general public does, that if they were really all that good they would have a manager. The second problem: It is exceedingly difficult, emotionally more than technically, to gracefully blow one's own horn, verbally rather than musically.

In dealing with the first of these, it may help to remember that the field is not fair. Demographics are against you, as stated before; there simply aren't enough openings on management rosters, or enough well-paying engagements, for everyone deserving of representation to get it. And miscarriages of justice do occur. You simply may not be the artistic flavor-of-the-month, or all the choice management opportunities in your field may be taken up for a number of years by others, perhaps, in your view, not as worthy as yourself - it happens all the time. This is not sufficient reason to deprive yourself of the chance for a fulfilling life in music, nor to deprive others of what you have musically to offer.

The second is a thornier problem. It may be most helpful to detour around the emotional question at first, and remember that there are learnable skills involved. Self-management is sales, and salesmanship is a learnable skill, which we will try to demonstrate in this chapter.

It's true that being a sufficiently good sales person to sell yourself requires enormous confidence, both to try it in the first place and to withstand the amount of rejection that you certainly will face. (A manager will experience as much rejection, by the way, but he can always feel that he's not being rejected - his client is.) A shift in your point of view may help you here; remember that some of the skills you have as a musician are applicable to management efforts. Effective performance is effective communication, and it is possible that you can communicate as effectively off stage as on. You can use what you already have as a performer, and try to generalize these skills to a broader arena.

Some self-management principles

- Keep in mind a clear idea of what you have to offer each potential sponsor.

- Be interested in others, listen to them carefully, & ask advice when you can.

- Assume a limited success rate, which, after all, is the norm in any business.

Realize that there are actually some advantages to self-managing over outside management. For one, you will actually be more attractive to some presenters because you'll be cheaper (no built-in commission to raise the fee). Some presenters, particularly the smaller ones, enjoy the personal contact with the artist. Also, you know what you have to offer, and may be better at describing it than someone else would be. Overall, you will be actively involved in your own career development, rather than feeling passive or powerless.

Now how do you get started?

Booking a date in four not-very-easy steps

In Bill Matthews' research, he found that most presenters at the level we're discussing expected to be called before being approached by mail. They explained that they receive so much unsolicited promotional material that unless they're expecting it, they'll pay little attention to a flyer or resume received in the mail. When you reach the person in charge of a performance series, they'll listen to you -it's actually their job.

Making phone calls is harder at first for most people than writing, though following the steps outlined below should help. If you're simply far too shy to make the initial approach by phone, or if you're dealing with presenters on a higher level who can't be reached by phone, a letter can be substituted; the same general format will do. At some point, though, you will need to use the phone for follow-up. (See step 3.)

Before you start, get together all the publicity materials you will need to send to the presenters when they request them, as they almost certainly will. It takes longer to get these together than you think, and you need to be prepared.

1. Whom do I call? Making a list of possibilities.

Make a list of possible places where you. might perform. In making the you will take into consideration:

- Where you have some kind of contact or connection,

- Who presents artists like yourself, or can be convinced to do so, and

- Where you would really like very much to play.

Almost everyone can come up with at least a short list based on one or some combination of the above. You might know that your alumni association has functions which might include live music; that the church you attended growing up, or the library in your home town, has a concert series; that your Aunt Sadie is on the board of directors of the local chamber music society. You might find a place where you performed as a kid on a special young person's concert, where they also hire professional artists. Any connection will get you at least a foot in the door, and will provide something concrete with which to start your dialogue.

A little research in the newspapers and other listings, such as the lists of presenters of concert series in the *Musical America Directory,* as well as conversations with colleagues, can also tell you about performance opportunities for which you might qualify. Lists of concert presenters are often obtainable for a fee from many state arts councils. Even a strong desire to perform on a particular series can provide you with an opening for discussion with the presenter. *Cold lists, however, should always be followed up with some research before you do your calling or writing;* such listings can be misleading, and you will waste time and money. CAG, for example, is listed as a presenter of a concert series in *Musical America,* and we do produce some; the concerts only include our competition winners and alumni, however, so the many letters we get every day from hopeful artists are simply thrown out, since there are too many of them to answer with a letter of clarification.

Laura Spitzer, who is cited in the chapter credits has assembled a "don't overlook" list of possible contacts. The sources from which she suggests creating a list of family, friends, friends of friends and acquaintances, some of which are mentioned above, include:

- Chamber of Commerce
- Parks and Recreation
- School District Offices, Principals, Teachers, Music Teachers, Parents and PTA Members
- Community Music Schools; School "Gifted and Talented" Programs
- Associations of Music Teachers
- Community, Junior, and Four Year Colleges and Universities
- Rotary, Kiwanis, Elks, Women's Clubs, other similar organizations
- Museums
- Churches
- Senior Citizen's Groups
- Institutions: Hospitals, Prisons, etc.
- Veteran's Groups
- Alumni Associations
- Music Stores
- Local and State Arts Councils

or even

- A business or corporation which might want to host an event, for employees, customers, etc.

Once you've got a list assembled, prepare to make a series of calls. Don't plan to make only one call, as the emotional investment should be amortized a bit by making several of them. And don't make your most important call - the engagement you want the most, or the one where you have the best chance of getting the job -first. After a few calls, you'll develop a certain fluency in your presentation, as well as a more devil-may-care attitude to either rejection or interest.

2. What should I say?

To get the person you want on the phone, use any introduction you can, preferably a real recommendation from a real person. If it is your Aunt Sadie, say so; if a fellow artist or another presenter whom the presenter knows suggested this venue, bring this up immediately. If you have no name to drop, bring up the connection which you've thought of, whether it is some geographical or historical association (as mentioned above) or simply a desire to perform at this hall.

Your first sentence (as above) will be said directly to the person you will want to talk to, or should get you in to talk to that person. Once you've got him on the phone, this sentence will become part of

The 20-Second Introduction

For the most part, you will reliably have someone's attention on the phone for about 20 seconds, at which point they will either want to hear more, or lose interest. **During that 20 seconds, you must say something which will buy you more time, and interest them in hiring you.**

This may sound dreadful, if you assume that you must sum up yourself and what you do in barely enough time to take a deep breath. But you don't. You simply have to establish that you have something worth hearing a bit more about. By starting the conversation with your connection, you're earning some extra seconds; without one, you have to have an even better opening. During the 20 seconds, you'll have to bring up either your most impressive credential to date, or the credential which will mean the most to this presenter.

When Bill Matthews is talking to a new presenter on the phone, for example, he says that he often begins by saying something like, "I'm a classical guitarist who has performed in over 65 countries around the world; most recently, I've returned from a tour of [China and other countries in the Far East.]" Bill has performed extensively as a Cultural Ambassador for the United States Information Agency, and feels that presenters are most impressed by the worldwide nature of his performance experience.

Other examples, made up by us. The format: first, a sentence or two to establish a connection; then, the crucial 20 seconds.

Example 1:

Establishing the connection:

"Hello, my name is -. [My Aunt Sadie, who is on your board of directors] [my friend Jill Hill, the pianist who performed on your series last year] [other reference] suggested that I call you about performing at [fill in name of sponsor]."

The 20 second introduction:

"I'm from Eastshore, and performed on the Eastshore Community Church young people's series years ago. Since then, I've gone on to become a professional musician, and perform dozens of concerts each year around the country; recently, for example, I performed a highly regarded concert at the Impressiveville Museum of Art. I would very much like to perform in my own region, and would love to come back to Eastshore as a performer on your regular series."

Note: The reference to the local connection and the *specific*, most impressive credential.

Example 2:

Establishing a reason for calling this venue (no personal connection, but a geographic one):

"Hello, I'm -. I'm a violinist, concertizing regularly in the Northeast, and I've spent summers here in Eastshore for several years."

The 20 second introduction:

"I've been a fan of your concert hall for years and attend your summer programs; since next season I'm doing other concerts in the area and I'll be here next summer as usual, I would like to perform on your series. I have a special program for families that I think would work well for your audience. "

Example 3:

>**Establishing a reason for calling** (no personal connection, no non-personal connection), **and going right on to the 20-second pitch.**
>
>"Hello, my name is -. I'm a singer, and I've just won the Interesting Artist of the Year Competition. I'm now seeking opportunities to bring the program with which I won that competition to a wider audience. I know that you produce a young artists' series, and I would be very interested in participating in it. "

Example 4:

>**Also combined, reason for calling and 20-second introduction:**
>
>"Hello, my name is -. I'm a clarinetist. Two years ago I graduated with some distinction from [Well Known Conservatory], and I've been performing extensively in [my area] since then. I would like to get some important exposure in other areas, and would very much like the opportunity to perform on your series."

This last is perhaps weakest, in that there is no specific credential or connection to interest the presenter; however, it can be a subtle way, if carefully worded, of saying in effect, "I can save you money; the exposure is worth more to me now than the fee."

Example 5:

>**The very best approach** is one not listed yet, since it goes,
>
>"Hi Fred, it's Ellen. I've got some free dates next year and a great new program I'd like to try out; any chance of working a concert into your season?"

In other words, the first name, we-already-know-each-other approach.

>Note that we assume, in all of these cases, that you are not at all famous, and that your programs are not startlingly unusual. If neither of these are true, so much the better - and the easier.

If you've captured enough of the presenter's attention to say a bit more, work in something about why your abilities and their needs would match well. This will show that you've done your homework, and also that you are interested in a successful concert, not just a gig. Concern for the presenter's success is much appreciated by them.

If the conversation runs long enough, and seems to be taking a positive course, mention some educational connection, if you do indeed have ability and experience in doing in-school performances or other events. Funding for concert series may be built around such school events, particularly in out-of-the-way communities.

> **Note:** This last bit of advice is given in the assumption that it isn't a school concert that you have been booking. But it is important to remember that much of your work, often by necessity in the earlier stages of your career and perhaps later on by choice and interest, will involve in-school performances, and many of your calls will be to book such events. Having expertise in this area is no longer simply an extra, enhancing one's performing possibilities, but a required and essential part of them. Make sure that you have at least two programs prepared, for K-5 and for 6-12 grade. Actively look for opportunities to try them out; not only will they form a source of income for you, but effective school programs will help make sure that there is an audience for your concerts in future years.

Back to booking the date:

At some point you may be requested to have your manager get in touch with the presenter, or simply asked directly why you are calling yourself. Have an answer ready. There are perfectly acceptable answers; you're just launching your career, and have not yet looked into the question of management; you're between managers; though several managers are interested in you, you've not yet decided which to go with, and don't want to halt your career while deciding; you might even have a manager, but prefer to work directly with the sponsors.

The fact is that with some presenters your credibility will depend on your having a manager, and with them this prejudice can't be completely overcome. But this won't always be true. Don't apologize, and don't feel - about this issue or any other - that you are at a disadvantage. It is this presenter's job to put together a concert series each year, and you do feel that you have a program which will be a positive addition to the series. The presenter will expect a confidence on your part that reflects your belief in your own abilities; you should be able to indicate this confidence while still being grateful for someone's interest and consideration.

During the course of this phone call, a relationship will begin to form; you will like each other, or not, and will find that you have things to talk about, or not. A degree of liking, apart from artistic considerations, is enormously important on both sides; if you have a good phone manner, it will clearly help, and if one person in your chamber ensemble is making these kinds of calls, please make sure that it is the most charming of you - or the one who enjoys talking to other people the most, which may be the same thing.

Also, keeping in mind principle two stated at the beginning of this chapter, that you should listen carefully - be on the alert for any mention by the presenter of some special feature regarding the series which you might work into your discussion. Laura Spitzer reminds her students to listen for the following and make notes during the course of the conversation: the presenter's profession, hobbies, name of spouse or children (I would add pets to that); anything about the profile of the organization, audience size, venue; certainly, their level of enthusiasm. You can use all this information in later calls.

The fee

If there's real interest, and you've gotten to the point of discussing brass tacks, the question of your fee will come up. The question may arise now, during the first call, or in the follow-up call, but, as it can be an uncomfortable issue to deal with, it's best to be prepared. Amounts mentioned will often turn out to be the final ones, even if discussed as "ball-park" figures.

It is fairly common for a presenter to make the first fee offer when dealing directly with an artist, but equally common for them to ask you what your fee is. This makes things difficult, of course, since your preferred answer to this question is probably, "As much as I can get." If you've done some homework beforehand, you might have gotten an idea of the fees paid by this presenter to other artists through asking around. If the series is funded by a local arts council or other public agency, you probably can get an idea of their fee range by calling that agency. (This information is usually public, though it may be complicated to get. An officer in the program which handles their grant application might be willing, informally, to give you some idea of the range, though they won't name specific fees to specific artists.)

You should also have some idea of how much you really need, weighing travel and other expenses against your need for exposure, experience and credentials, thus establishing a bottom line below which you can't afford to go. Don't be too afraid that you won't be taken seriously if you don't stick to a high fee; you can always state some reason why you'd make an exception, just for them and just this once. You're trying out a program, you want a foot in the door in this community, you will almost certainly have engagements in the area right around that time; all are good reasons which the presenter will accept.

Finally, you can always say, "My usual fee is $ (some figure)..." followed by a pause or a full stop. The stop puts the ball in their court, and it's left to them to explain why theirs is not a "usual" case. If it feels wrong to leave it at that, consider adding, after your pause, "... but this is negotiable, since I realize that you might find it difficult to go that high." Or something to that effect.

To give you some ball-park figures: Fees of $1,000 to $3,000 for a young solo artist are considered reasonable for most serious touring engagements, depending on the artist's credentials and the series' budget. Libraries and similar community venues will not pay fees even close to this level, but they do offer opportunities for warm-ups, trying out programs and gaining experience that may make up for the small fees.

3. Following the initial call

Now, one of two things will probably happen. The most likely is that the presenter is either mildly interested, or not interested but not unfeeling (or honest) enough to simply say so; almost certainly what she will say is, "Please send me some materials that I can look over. *You must, at this point, be ready to immediately - that is, at the most within a couple of days, before she forgets who you are -send out very good publicity materials, including a flyer if you have one, or a picture and biography if you don't, reviews, feature articles if you have them, plus a short cover letter referring to your conversation and reiterating the important points.* Hand write this if your handwriting is good. Otherwise, make sure it's not a form letter, hand sign it, and make sure the presenter's name and title are spelled right. It is exceedingly important that your materials be very slick and professional looking, and that you send them out quickly; one reason that presenters are afraid to deal with artists without managers is that they're afraid the artists will be difficult to deal with in one way or another. Good looking materials say that you're a first class artist; prompt correspondence says that you take care of business. Don't send a CD at this point, unless specifically asked for one (reason below).

In the event that there is no interest and the presenter actually says so, don't miss the opportunity to ask if she can recommend anyone else whom you might call. Principle number two, asking advice when you can, comes into its own here. Give the presenter the opportunity to be generous; she will often open up, particularly if she's just turned you down, and feels a bit bad about it. If she does refer you to a colleague, you will have accomplished several things: first, you'll have a personal connection, a name to drop, in your next call; second, you will be moving closer to your target, a venue that is actually right for you, where you have a shot at getting a performance.

There is a third, and very unlikely, possibility: that the presenter will be so impressed with your presentation, or your reputation will have preceded you and they know you so well already, that you get a positive response immediately. If this happens, skip to the end of the next section.

4. The follow-up call and beyond

Let's now suppose that you've been asked for materials and have sent them, and two weeks have gone by. You're now entitled to make a follow-up call. The real purpose of the call is to ask whether the sponsor now wants to hire you, but you can't ask that directly, and probably things aren't that simple anyway. You therefore must be prepared with something to say (not just "have the materials have arrived safely"), or something specific to offer. If you are performing in the general area, you might invite him; if you have accomplished something in the interim, such as a competition win or a successful concert, you should tell the presenter about it. Otherwise, now's the time to offer a CD (this is one reason why you didn't send one before; the other is that CDs are too expensive to send to those who aren't really interested in listening to them).

Another item which you probably should bring up in this phone call, or possibly in the previous one, is, "When do you start scheduling your concerts for the coming season, and when should I be in touch again?" This will often set up your follow-up schedule for the next call, and help you to be most effective with this presenter in the future.

A second follow-up call is all right, but more than that is silly. If no deal has been cut by this time, or if no time schedule has been set up for further negotiation ("We've already got next season's schedule set, but call me in the fall about the season after that and let's talk again"), drop the phone calls for a while, but remember to keep the presenter posted on your current activities through periodic (perhaps no more than yearly) notes with reviews, invitations to your other concerts and the like.

What to do if you've got the date

When a deal is made, you should send out a letter confirming it. You could send out a more formal contract, if you wish (a sample contract follows at the end of this chapter), or the presenter may have a standard form that they use. Whether you use a contract or a letter, it should clearly state the financial terms of the deal, the times involved and the division of responsibilities. With a contract, send two copies for their signature, sign one to return to them for their files and keep one yourself.

When the time comes for the concert to take place, taking the following advice will make it more likely that you'll be re-engaged someday, apart from how well the actual performance goes:

Make sure that flyers or other materials have gotten to the presenter in plenty of time (ask them what plenty of time means, and make sure you stick to the timetable), and that they're of excellent quality. Similarly, give them program information as promptly as possible; if you can't decide on a program, send your best guess. If there must be later changes, so be it. (Be careful, though; some presenters in some regions are *seriously* offended by changes, whereas others think that the informality of last minute changes is perfectly fine. If an artist happens to have a tour in Japan, for example, such last minute changes are regarded as discourteous and disorganized, and are a major gaffe.)

Call a few days before the concert, to make sure that all is well.

Come early. Never give a presenter a heart attack by walking in a few minutes before the downbeat.

Help the presenter by making yourself available for newspaper interviews, radio broadcasts or other public relations opportunities, and to the community for before-concert events.

Attend the post-concert reception, and check with the presenter to see if there's anyone that you should be particularly careful to thank.

Be easy to work with, and flexible about your times and working conditions (within reason).

Talk to the audience if you're good at it, and if the concert situation is informal enough to make it appropriate.

Be sensitive overall to the presenter's concerns. Each event for her is like being the host of a party, with all of the anxieties associated with important social, as well as business, events. She wants it to be a success, and you can help.

Some general guidelines, from Laura

The following ideas - not in any priority order - are drawn from Laura's notes for her classes and from talks she's given on self-management.

• Don't ever expect anyone to call you back, and never take lack of response personally.

• Her advice regarding fees: If a presenter cannot meet your asking fee, offer to throw in another school program or service for free, pointing out the revenue this can generate to make up the difference; reduce your fee only as a last resort.

• Never back a presenter into a corner; give them lots of room [and time] to talk and think things over and make relaxed decisions.

• Repeat dates and times over the phone, and again on paper when you write; send contracts as soon as possible, to avoid any misunderstandings.

• Use a booking address that will not change, at least for a few years. In some cases, a P.O. box is the best way to do this.

• Reorder materials before you run out.

• Keep an audience mailing list, by putting a sign-up sheet out at every concert; send them notices about recordings or a performances, or copies of articles that appear about you.

• Overestimate travel time.

• Always assume that your audience is highly intelligent, and don't be fooled by clothes or manner that you think indicates the contrary. The more sensitive you believe your audience to be, the more they will respond to you and rise to your expectations.

Please read this: a final, very important note.

Since forewarned is at least a step towards being forearmed, here are some important thoughts to inform your longer-term perspective. First, none of the performers that we have ever spoken with really likes being his own manager. All said that they would prefer having a *good* manager to being self-managed. But the crucial word *is good;* many artists are dissatisfied with their managers, and some, making a virtue of necessity, find self-management to be preferable. At least one effectively self-managed artist contacted said that, though he would rather have a big, powerful management than be running his own operation, he got no better results when he was with one of the smaller, less powerful ones than he now gets on his own. This is not to say that small managements are ineffective, but rather that the difference in success, for him at least, comes not from management as opposed to self-management, but from effective self-management as opposed to not-as-effective outside management.

Laura notes that it probably takes about 10 years to get a career rolling, and that starting out knowing this will help sustain you through the tough times.

She adds that the motivation which fuels this effort is a talent separate from musical gifts, but perhaps as important in predicting how successful your efforts will be. In her own words,

> "Talent being equal, how would you answer these questions: Out of ten apathetic, passive, inarticulate, depressive musicians, how many will make it? or, Out of ten enthusiastic, tenacious, driven, verbal, optimistic musicians, how many will make it?"

Laura is a highly unusual person, who is the second kind of musician much of the time. The rest of us are the first kind of musician some days, the second kind other days, and somewhere in between in general. If you tend toward type two though, your chances of being able to sustain your self-management efforts, particularly during difficult times, are improved.

In this regard, it is wise to keep in mind that a self-managed free-lance career as a musician usually has a maximum life span: perhaps the 10 or so years mentioned above. At this point, most people need to have built up sufficient momentum to change the balance from them doing most of the calling to mostly being called: or they start to change the way they live, to look for different and more steady work in the field, or to consider doing something else entirely. And they may make such changes even if their careers are going pretty well.

There are several reasons for this. First, self-managed free-lance careers are really, really hard. Though there are remarkable individuals who are exceptions to the rule, most people can't keep up the level of positive energy and unremitting effort required to maintain and consistently build a career, without much help, for longer than this, and sometimes not for this long - even though expecting a career to take off in a shorter period may be unrealistic.

Second, the self-managed free-lance career is very rarely lucrative, even when the musician is booking an enviable number of dates for himself; the expenses of touring can be high, the level of fee hardly princely, and the amount of unpaid time and effort spent on one°s own behalf enormous. Usually, the ratio of gross income to net income, that is, how much of the fees you get you actually have as income, is about 3 to 1, or even 2 to 1, for the typical touring performer. That means that if you gross $30,000 in fees - which many artists would think is respectable -you rarely will clear more than $10-15,000 of this. One pianist we know, who earned a very respectable gross income of $77,000 one year performing almost 100 self-booked concerts (some of them school concerts linked to larger performances), realized a net income of just over $16,000 after expenses, due to the extraordinary costs involved in that particular year of travel, plus things like upkeep on his piano. (He noted that he would have earned more bagging groceries.)

During the period when a young artist is investing in her own future, though, it's an investment, and that may be enough (supplemented by some kind of part time teaching or a day job); but in the long run, or when life, in the form of spouses or children or other interests or responsibilities, makes its presence known, it is not enough to sustain either body or soul.

But consider the alternative. If you want to perform enough, and are willing to put in at least a few years, it's worth a shot. It's also not entirely unpleasant; there are rewards, and from time to time it can be both challenging and actually fun to tackle and solve the problem of getting yourself some work. And as an alternative, either from the beginning or when you simply can't do it all yourself anymore, it is possible to hire and train someone to do all, or part, of the work for you. Remember though that in most cases this can be done effectively only when you already have some self-management experience, and can train the person you hire by drawing on that experience. Make sure, if you take this route, that your representative will be as effective as you would be - or more so.

Help for artists interested in school performances

Educational Outreach programs have flourished in recent years, and represents a more important source of income for many young musicians. One way to keep up with new developments is though a new journal established by Eric Booth entitled *Teaching Artist Journal: A Quarterly Forum for Professionals*.

Sample Artist/Presenter Contract

Agreement date: January 15, 2003   Engagement date: January 15, 2004

AGREEMENT between XYZ RECITAL SERIES (hereunder "SPONSOR") and JOE ARTIST (hereunder "ARTIST").

1.   SPONSOR engages ARTIST, and ARTIST agrees to perform a recital on Monday, January 15, 2003 at 8:00 p.m. in Anytown, USA for a fee of $2500.00.

2.   Payment by SPONSOR of the fee of $2500.00, in the form of a company or organization check payable to "Joe Artist," is to be presented to ARTIST or mailed or delivered to ARTIST immediately following the conclusion of the performance. No deduction from the fee set forth herein shall be made by SPONSOR for performance rights fees, or for any other purpose, other than all applicable and customarily deducted taxes, without prior written consent of ARTIST.

3.   SPONSOR agrees, at SPONSOR's expense, to furnish the hall for the engagement herein contracted. The hall is to be well heated and lighted, clean and in good order, with all necessary ushers, ticket collectors, licenses, and clean dressing room for ARTIST and any assisting artists provided. SPONSOR further agrees to make the hall available to ARTIST prior to the performance for rehearsal at a time previously agreed upon as acceptable to both ARTIST and SPONSOR. The house piano is to be in excellent condition and properly tuned.

4.   ARTIST will furnish to SPONSOR a copy of the program to be performed. SPONSOR agrees, at SPONSOR's expense, to print and distribute a sufficient quantity of house programs in conformity with the material furnished by ARTIST. SPONSOR agrees to print on all programs, immediately after the musical portion, the following: "Joe Artist records for ABC Records."

5.   SPONSOR agrees to arrange, at SPONSOR'S expense, for a page turner to be available for the performance should ARTIST request it. ARTIST agrees to notify SPONSOR of such request at least two weeks in advance of the performance.

(Sample Artist/Presenter Contract, continued)

6.   ARTIST agrees to provide SPONSOR with press materials and flyers in quantities ARTIST feels sufficient. SPONSOR must place the request for these materials at least five weeks prior to the date of engagement, and agrees to pay all applicable shipping charges in the event of a request for very large quantities or a rush order. SPONSOR further agrees to properly distribute and display all advertising material received and to return unused materials.

7.   ARTIST shall not be under any liability for failure of ARTIST to appear or perform for any cause beyond ARTIST's control, including, but not limited to, illness or accident, regulations of public authorities, labor difficulties, civil tumult, strike, epidemic, and interruption or delay of transportation service. In the event that ARTIST defaults for reasons beyond ARTIST'S control, SPONSOR will not be responsible for the payment of the fees agreed to in this contract, and ARTIST will refund any moneys already paid. Neither will ARTIST be responsible for any of SPONSOR's costs, already incurred or otherwise, for the local production and publicity of the events. Further, ARTIST and SPONSOR agree to make every effort to reschedule the events for a mutually agreeable date.

8.   SPONSOR agrees to prevent the broadcast, recording, or reproduction, by radio, television, or any other device, of ARTIST'S performance, or any part thereof, without the specific written consent of ARTIST. SPONSOR agrees that the engagement shall not be a joint recital, nor shall any assisting artist perform without prior consent of ARTIST.

9.   This agreement shall not be binding on ARTIST until executed by ARTIST. This agreement represents the full understanding between the parties, and ARTIST shall not be bound by any terms or undertakings not contained herein. This agreement may not be assigned by SPONSOR, but shall be binding on SPONSOR and SPONSOR'S personal representative and successors.

_____   _____
JOE ARTIST   *XYZ RECITAL SERIES*

_____   _____
DATE   *DATE*

IX. All of the Above for Composers

Many ideas in this chapter came from conversations with composers Oliver Knussen and Marc Neikrug. We talked extensively with these two because they've chosen lives which combine performance and composing in a fashion which contributes significantly to the field; the reader will come to see that this is a path we very much believe in. Also very helpful in gathering points of view for the chapter were composer and former director of the Career Planning and Placement Office at the Manhattan School of Music, Mark LaPorta; Vice President and Director of Promotions at G. Schirmer, Inc. Susan Feder; Boosey & Hawkes' President Jennifer Bilfield; pianists and champions of new music Alan Feinberg and Ursula Oppens; and many other composers, too numerous to cite here.

This chapter contains much information that you would expect, and doesn't include some information that you might expect. Trying to avoid duplication, we have chosen not to include information on performing rights, for example, which are better covered by the performing rights organizations themselves, or in Meet the Composer's handbook by Lauren Iossa and Ruth Dreier, Composers in the Marketplace: How to Earn a Living Writing Music. *The same is true for contracts, commission fees and arrangements, and more. We've chosen to devote the space to topics not addressed, or not addressed in depth, by other organizations in the field.*

Everything stated in the previous chapters about performers - that is, needing to understand your own musical identity, being able to communicate it to the world, creating supportive networks, etc. - is equally true for composers. But composers often have an even more difficult time of it, for a number of reasons. First, the composer not only often lacks the most basic information about career development, but has fewer resources for learning about what it entails. Second, the composer is usually in the background, rather than out there for everyone to see and admire.

A few ideas which have informed our point of view, and which you might keep in mind as you make your way through this chapter.

- **You need to get out into the field**, creating professional equity against which you can draw support and loyalty.

- **You need to be prepared** with appropriate and clear materials as soon as possible.
- **You need to develop skills** for dealing effectively with performers, colleagues in the field, and audiences.
- **You need to support your fellow composers.**

A chief problem for composers is isolation: an isolation that can cut them off from their potential audiences, supporters, collaborators, interpreters - even from composer colleagues. It can be psychologically very difficult. (Oliver Knussen says, "Decide how much you want to be alone; composing is an emotion-numbingly lonely occupation. It's also extremely labor intensive, or should be.") And this isolation can, at worst, separate the composer from new and sustaining sources of musical thought and growth.

But that is a topic for another book. Our concern here is that isolation not only keeps composers hidden from view, it puts them in the position - in relation to the rest of the field - of asking for help, rather than in a relationship involving reciprocity and mutual support.

Accepting that composers need, one way or another, to be players in the game rather than onlookers on the periphery, one way is to perform, and this is the way we'll discuss first. (Further along in the chapter we'll deal with other ways of both contributing to and participating in the musical life of the community.) Through performance composers can become advocates *for themselves and for others,* find satisfying musical partners, and make important musical alliances.

Performing and Composing

We don't seem to live in a time when composers are also virtuoso performers, as in the nineteenth century. Even those composers who conduct and who are, for example, also terrific pianists - Lukas Foss, Andre Previn, and the late Leonard Bernstein come to mind - don't write primarily for themselves, or even primarily for the piano.

For a few composers, though, starting and performing in an ensemble which exclusively performs that composer's music has been the path to considerable success, and the means by which they've found their public (as Philip Glass and Steve Reich have done). An equally successful model is provided by composers who start and/or perform in chamber ensembles which play a wide variety of new music, or of both new and older music. Composer Joan Tower, for example, was pianist for many years with the Da Capo Chamber Players, for which she wrote and premiered several important works, as well as performed the works of fellow composers.

Composers can make a performance opportunity which isn't exclusively theirs, and which they haven't started, their principal compositional vehicle as well. Composer Don York, former music director for the Paul Taylor dance company, has written several orchestral works for the company, all of which have gotten significant exposure both in the company's home base and on tour.

Two of the composers interviewed for this chapter have been particularly active as performers, in different ways. Oliver Knussen has been conducting almost as long as he's been composing. Though he often conducts his own music, he has been an indefatigable champion of the music of his fellow composers. This advocacy, added to his compositional gifts and his very wide-ranging musical curiosity and knowledge, has consistently brought him the respect and attention of the field. Composer Marc Neikrug chose a life in which performance, separate for the most part from his compositional activity, was primary for a long time in terms of making a living and visibility. As half of a violin and piano duo (Neikrug performs with Pinchas Zukerman), he has had a wide experience of the field, has learned how it works and has made friends. In his own words:

"From the beginning I wanted to perform as well as compose. For a composer like me - who isn't the compositional equivalent of a 9 to 5er, and doesn't absolutely need to compose every day - this is the perfect job. I know my schedule way ahead of time, so I can plan when I can write (the minimum amount of time I need for getting back into composing, some down time, and producing some work, is three weeks). Being part of a duo was a specific choice; the enormous repertoire and the memorization required of a solo pianist would require more hours than would allow me to compose. I do some solo playing, and some conducting, but limit the amount. It's easier to go from composing to performing than the other way around, when I need time to get all the other notes out of my head before working on my own.

"There's always been an enormous pressure from outside to choose, to be one thing or another. I feel they're all one piece; I couldn't play the way I play if I wasn't a composer. It's probably equally true that being a performer affects the music I write; but neither is extricable from the other."

A very important note: Knussen reminds us that performing can be a way of learning, growing and maintaining an active involvement with the field *without bringing one's music before the public before it's ready*. He says:

"Many young composers are desperately anxious to be seen and recognized publicly, rather than to work hard at their musical growth. No status should be attached to being known until you are seriously convinced that the music is really ready to be heard."

Not performing ... but out in the field

A composer's living, while she's young, will almost never come primarily from composition. It probably won't come from composition even to the extent that a fledgling performer, who's free lancing and being actively entrepreneurial about creating performance opportunities for herself, will make some of her living from performing. (Royalties, rental fees, etc. for composers under fifty add up to very little money, with a few exceptions; commissions can pay very good money, but unless the composer has lined up a string of them, lasting several years, she will have to earn at least part of her living doing something else.)

However, the composer's living, if at all possible, should come from activities which teach him useful things about the field, and which create contacts with people and organizations. In general this book does not deal with vocational guidance, but we can propose some possibilities.

We've just suggested:

- developing your performing skills, and playing the music of other composers;
- learning to conduct, and conducting other people's music as well as your own;
- starting a performing group in which you are a performer, conductor, and/or *administrator*.

We haven't discussed the last of these yet, but you can certainly start, or participate in starting, a performing ensemble or concert series without actually performing in it; all these groups need administration, and someone who's energetic, devoted and organized is beyond price. You could, moreover, be the group's in-house composer-in-residence.

By forming a local composer's alliance for example, and starting a concert series as one activity of the alliance, you could be involved with making music happen in a very important way. The example of Libby Larson, and Stephen Paulus, and the Minnesota Composer's Forum (now the American Composers Forum) demonstrates how effective such organizations can become, both for the field and for those that put so much effort into them. This model is particularly useful in smaller cities where such resources for composers don't already exist.

Of course, in order to get to do any of these, you will need to follow the guidance laid out for performers in previous chapters. It won't be easy, but it probably will be worth the effort.

Alternatively (or in addition), you could

- Work with a radio station as a programmer; or with a music festival or other performing organization in artistic administration. You'll meet lots of people, including performers, and learn a lot about reaching audiences. You can use your extensive knowledge of the repertoire (which you have, of course) to make a difference in what's being listened to, and to become an advocate for your part of the field. But be prepared to keep quiet about your own work unless asked about it.

- Work with **ASCAP or BMI,** or some other kind of composer's organization. These offer opportunities for very good networking, and you can develop an understanding of basic mechanisms of the business.

- Start your own publishing company or record label. This sounds very ambitious, and would certainly take some fairly serious, up-front money, but - if you can make the investment, and have the right personality - they're interesting ways of bringing the world to you, instead of the other way around.

An old friend of this author is a composer, primarily of band music. Being of an organizational turn of mind, interested in computers, and having few other options at that point in his life anyway, he bought himself a computer and the appropriate software and started to self-publish, developing a list of band directors around the country and marketing his work directly to them. He was amazingly successful on many fronts: his band music began to get known and played, he got commissions from some loyal customers after a while (including several for non-band music), he began to publish the works of other composers that interested him, and now has something of a small corner on this part of the market. The financial rewards were pretty slow in coming, but other rewards - contacts, commissions, travel, etc. - grew quite steadily. The same principle could apply to starting a record label, though the marketing would be much more difficult (not that the publishing business was easy), and the income likely to be close to non-existent, since the overhead costs can be so high. Several composers we know are recording engineers, however, and work with other composers on producing independent records for them, which is another interesting way of combining learning and getting around with income.

• Working as a critic or otherwise writing about music. This is an interesting possibility, with a distinguished history, though not one much in fashion now. We do know one or two, though, who have pursued this path. It would be good to see more active musicians involved in writing about music for the general public.

• And more and more. Internships in public relations & marketing, with an orchestra perhaps? You'll learn about how music is marketed; frightening, perhaps, but definitely interesting. An internship in development with some arts organization, not even necessarily a musical one? You will certainly learn to define and pitch a project. Also, remember that joining national composer's organizations, like the American Music Center, will keep you in touch with information about opportunities in the field and bring you together with your colleagues.

All this gets the composer "grounded," and helps him to learn the languages of other parts of the field. These ideas also represent a way of developing a place in the business in which *he can be of help to other musicians,* both performers and composers.

What about teaching?

Composers have always taught, and rightly so, both in and out of the academy. Academic jobs, though, are getting harder and harder to come by, so the university or conservatory as home base for the composer's career is an option for fewer individuals than it once was. This chapter deals principally with skills which the composer should develop and which will enhance all sorts of job opportunities -teaching included. If you love to teach, and should you find yourself with a conservatory or college teaching job (or any teaching job, for that matter), developing other sides of your professional life will not only add to your teaching effectiveness (and employability), but can help guard against a comfortable descent into the isolation which this chapter is trying to help you avoid.

Developing skills & learning about the field, early on: Perhaps while in school

Composers need to start early developing strong, supportive collegial relationships *with performers and with fellow composers.* You need to support their work while in school, and remain active as a supporter of their work when you're out. You need to develop the performance skills you will need throughout your musical life - particularly conducting, since the period in one's life when one can round up a group of musicians on a voluntary basis and convince them to let you lead them is short, and likely to be when you (and, more important, they) are younger rather than older. You need to get out and around, to hear as much as you can. And, obviously, you need to develop your own musical voice.

Knussen:

"For some players that you genuinely get on with personally, and some you respect, start an ensemble and get them to teach you to conduct. Don't think of it as a performing ensemble, but rather as a place for everybody to try to learn new things.

"My recipe for learning how to be a decent composer is to investigate as many different ways as possible of doing what interests you. Find out what you want to do, and utilize whatever you've got in your technical arsenal to achieve an end result which is the most meaningful and practical realization of what you want to say. Find an actual, active professional composer who has a musical life outside the university, and apprentice yourself for a bit. Offer to do odd jobs, copying or proofreading, anything that needs doing. It's an old fashioned way, but probably the best. He is more likely to talk to you about the things which actually engage him while composing, rather than give you a composition lesson. The best mentor is someone who can do something you can't, or who works in a way that you don't understand but that you respect and admire.

"Make as many contacts with as many composers of as many different backgrounds as possible. That's why a place like Tanglewood is so useful; you can learn a lot about what you want to do as a composer, through a process of elimination if nothing else, and through the cross-fertilization of ideas which can happen there. Going to a festival or studying with a particular composer for the sake of a line on your resume, isn't worth it.

"[Get to] know the literature well. Your knowledge will make you valuable as a resource for conductors, etc., and will be useful to you as composer-inresidence."

Neikrug:

"You have to make composing your work, instead of cutting yourself off from the field. To do that, you must a) play something, play it as well as you can, and perform, and 2) talk, think and understand your fellow musicians. You certainly have to identify with performers; you can't presume to write a phrase of music without having played one."

"Students need to get out to hear music from outside; they need to go hear the Guarneri Quartet, and to go backstage and congratulate them, as well as the school concerts. You have to get into the field, and meet people. When I met the composer Bright Sheng recently, he reminded me that we had met ten years earlier when he had turned pages for me at a concert at BAM, and that we had had an interesting conversation about my music. What a great way to meet lots of people that you might not meet otherwise! People can always use page turners."

A few suggestions from the publishers with whom we spoke, as to what advice they might give to young composers, particularly while in school. First, from Susan Feder of G. Schirmer:

- Cultivate performance contacts, and get good taped material.
- Understand what performers need and can do, and develop sensitivity to their needs; the clearer your performance materials, the better chance you have for a good performance.
- Learn to conduct, or to perform yourself.
- Take time to learn your craft; really learn orchestration, etc. Often less is more.

And, from a former Boosey & Hawkes vice-president:

- Take classes in notation skills and the like, things that you won't be able to get easily after you're out.
- Try to be active in the music organizations of the school - perhaps as ensemble librarian, to work with scores, parts and players.
- Start an ensemble, or a festival, in or out of school. "Bang on a Can" has been both an exciting festival in itself and a wonderful vehicle for the three composers who started it (David Lang, Michael Gordon and Julia Wolfe).

Even if it's not so early ... Some general advice

Neikrug:
"I was fortunate; my father played my work, his students played my work. You will need someone of some stature to perform something, anything of yours; that gives you credibility. But you still have to hang around. Go to everyone's concerts, shake everyone's hand. When the time comes, they'll need a new piece - who they commission depends a lot on who pops into their head, often the last composer they spoke to. I did that for years. I never asked anyone to play a piece of mine, and never talked -on those occasions - about my music. But I was there. *Musicians are not interested in new pieces. They are interested in somebody they like. Nobody asks to hear or see some of your music when they learn you're a composer (correction: players who don't have much repertoire for their instrument or ensemble will ask); they ask after they've heard something.*

"When you're starting out, you can never say 'no, I don't have that,' or 'I can't do that.' I got my first major performance and acquired a publisher at the same time. My piano teacher was playing with an orchestra, and told the conductor about me. The conductor asked if I had written a piano concerto (I said yes though I hadn't) which I could play. He then said that if I had a publisher who would supply him with parts (I said yes, though I didn't), he would perform it. I then went to Barenreiter, and asked if they would publish [parts to] my piano concerto (!); they said yes if I had a guaranteed performance, which I told them I did. When I was at Marlboro a similar incident happened. I walked in on some percussion players who were setting up to rehearse; they asked if I had a percussion piece, because they would play it if I did. I said I would in three days."

"It's important to see your career as a long trajectory. You probably can't make most of your living from composing when you're young, but if you look at the longer view, perhaps it can be increasingly how you make your living as you go along."

Knussen:
"If you're interested in writing orchestral and/or instrumental music, get yourself into as many orchestra rehearsals as possible (three times a week if you can). If you're interested in opera, write to the company's artistic administrator and ask if you can attend rehearsals.

"Don't be cowed by what everyone tells you to do. Doing other things can be helpful. Resist the temptation to write endless pieces d'occasion for money; hold out rather for working longer at a more major, more useful work. "

Regarding this last issue; note that although Knussen warns against writing many pieces *d'occasion*, Marc Neikrug states that you should never say "no" to an opportunity when you're starting out - and many of these opportunities will likely be to write pieces *d'occasion*. These are very personal and equally legitimate ways of thinking about one's work, and either can be applied with wisdom to a particular phase in one's career - or to a particular composer.

It is important that composers realize that at first, at least, and perhaps in the longer run as well, they will often be writing for their friends, who will be their primary source of encouragement, inspiration and opportunities. And what their friends want may be easily programmable ten to twelve minute works. If your friends need these short pieces, don't reject writing them out of hand - unless it's absolutely the wrong thing for you musically. Only you can determine this.

Working with performers

Some kind of guidance about proper etiquette when working with performers is badly needed by many composers, certainly and most desperately by those not actually performers themselves. A few tips, from our interviewees:

Knussen:

"If you're young, it's a safe bet to assume that everyone in the room knows more about what they're doing than you do. It's also safe to assume that if you've done your best with preparing materials, and if the notation of the piece is considerately done, chances are the players will be sympathetic to you. Chances are also that advice from them, if given, will be constructive. You don't waste their time, and they don't waste yours.

"Do not expect performers to like everything they're playing. You can hope that they will, but it's highly unlikely that that will be true. Do not walk in defensively or react with hostility. Accept advice graciously. If you hear a wrong note, or many, wait until the passage has been played through at least once and perhaps twice more before diplomatically pointing it out. Then point out quietly but unambiguously that you think there may be an error.

"It may be that some players detest the kind of music that you write, or generally have an attitude problem. This is not your problem. Respond quietly but unambiguously.

"Choose your words very carefully. When a trumpet player asks what kind of mute you want, don't respond, ' well in the last performance the player used a blue one.' If necessary, say ' I'm not sure' and ask for advice. (There's no shame in honesty!)

"Let them play. Don't fuss about minutiae. Don't say, 'Yes, of course, I know that.' If there's a genuine problem, having to do with materials or something that really doesn't work, encourage the conductor or leader to leave it alone, and sort it out yourself before the next rehearsal. Less talk the better. Don't stop the conductor or leader with details during the session; keep a list and hand it to him/her in plenty of time for the next rehearsal. If you don't think this will work, transfer the items to index cards, and supplement the list handed to the conductor with placing the cards on the appropriate players stands."

Sending scores and CDs to performers

This is purely a matter of simple common sense and politeness. **Don't ever send an unsolicited score without some kind of introduction, or at least without some strong reason to believe that your work would be of interest to this particular performer.** Include a cover letter which reminds the performer of this connection, and thank him for his interest in your work. If you want your materials sent back, enclose a self-addressed return envelope with enough postage - and don't expect things to be returned quickly, even then. People are busy. Make sure that the score you send is completely clean and legible (in these days of computer copying, no one is really willing to deal with difficult to decipher scores anymore), and that the tape or CD is of good quality. Let the performer know what you can easily provide in addition: if you have a clean set of parts on hand, for example.

Pianist Alan Feinberg gets unsolicited scores all the time, and tries very hard to look at them all. He doesn't always succeed, and doesn't always manage to send them back. He actually has done something with unsolicited material every once in a while though, which contradicts what has been said above; he's programmed works, forwarded scores on to other artists, or gotten to know a composer's work from scores or CDs sent cold. But he's unusually conscientious about this sort of thing, and these happy results have not occurred often.

He describes a recent scenario which did turn him off, however, which might provide a cautionary tale for you. A composer came up to congratulate him after a performance, and to ask if it would be all right to send him a score, to which he replied that it would be fine. A score to a piano concerto arrived at his manager's office soon thereafter, with a cover letter which stated that this piece had the interest of a particular conductor, though it didn't mention whether the conductor was interested in Alan as well; and that there was a European recording planned, with another pianist. A few weeks later, the composer called Alan, to ask if he was interested. In regard to what performance? Evidently this composer rather expected that, if he were interested, he would make a performance happen.

The problem here is that the composer seemed to have no idea in the world what the performer's life is like. He had assumed that if Alan liked it, this piece would, or could, immediately rise to the top of Alan's "to do" list, ignoring works and composers that he's wanted to program for a long time. He assumed that finding a performance opportunity was Alan's responsibility, and that it wouldn't be too difficult: when the actuality is that there aren't that many opportunities within most performer's schedules to insert another work (or to find a concerto performance at all), that most presenters know what they want to have performed (at least generally), and there is often not much flexibility. It also assumed the wrong relationship: that is, that the composer asks for help, and the performer gives it. Had the composer had something specific to bring to the table - an actual performance or recording opportunity to offer, for example - the reaction might have been different. Without something specific, the score should have been sent purely to let Alan get acquainted with the composer's work, and the follow-up call simply a thank you for his looking at it.

Pianist Ursula Oppens adds that the reverse - that is, being offered something, but for the wrong reasons - can be a total turn-off as well. She speaks of getting a call from a composer asking if she would play a piece of his on a concert in New York. He said he had a CD which he could send her, which was quite good; when she asked why he wasn't asking the pianist on the CD to perform, he responded that she [Ursula] was more famous. This was bad. Loyalty in the field is much prized, and composers and performers develop mutually rewarding relationships which sustain them both. Stepping over loyal supporters in search of greater glory is noticed, and usually deplored.

Publishers

The role of a good publisher in a composer's life can be analogous to that of a good manager in a performer's: that is, they can do an enormous amount of administrative work for you, get your music around and played, and work with you on career development. However, it is as difficult to get a good publisher as it is for performers to get a good manager, and there is some question as to why,

194

as well as when, you need one, given changes in the technology and finances of the publishing world over the last decade or two.

Before going into the composer's views on publishers, here are interviews with the representatives of two major, respected publishers, with the basics of the business. The author's questions are in italics.

Susan Feder, Vice President, G. Schirmer Inc.

How does a composer get on your roster?

Feder:

"We go to a great many concerts, and may be intrigued by someone's work that we've heard; alternatively, we may get a call from someone in the business recommending a particular composer. Some recommendations come from composers already on our list. We do listen to unsolicited submissions of scores or tapes on a regular basis, but it's rare that we find composers to add to the roster that way. When there's interest in particular composers, we go to their concerts, meet with them to get a sense of them not only as musicians but as people - as well as to learn about their career expectations and goals as well as to develop a publishing and promotional strategy. Schirmer doesn't want to take a composer on for whom we can't make a real difference in their career development.

We do look for composers with an interesting, original perspective. We recognize that we are in a mufti-cultural, ethnically diverse world, and are looking for music that reflects this. We also often take into account the views of our colleagues in our sister companies around the world who can bring artistic perspective to our deliberations."

Who's 'WE'?

Feder:

"The Editorial Committee consists of our directors of publications and rentals, members of the promotion department, and me. All form a kind of A&R *(Artists and Repertoire)* team."

What is the role the publisher plays in the life of a composer under exclusive contract?

Feder:

"The publisher frees composers to do what they do best: compose. The publisher protects the composer's copyrights worldwide, negotiates fees, and promotes the composer by looking for commissions, performances, recordings, and film opportunities; prepares, stores and distributes performing materials and printed publications; dispenses advice; and strategizes career development. Very much like management for performers.

"We also see the publisher as an information service on behalf of the composer, providing program notes, keeping track of reviews and performances, etc. We were the first classical music publisher to develop an active presence on the Internet, so much of this information is being disseminated electronically, and to markets we might not have reached otherwise. G. Schirmer is part of the Music Sales Group, an international company with offices worldwide, so we are able to offer promotion and administration that is at once international and localized.

"The printing of scores is less important than it once was; primarily it has promotional value. We do take seriously the archival importance of the printed score; in years to come, it is important that someone be able to see what the music was that Schirmer considered important at any given moment in musical history. Most printed scores of new music don't sell enough to make money; sometimes the publisher can anthologize particular works, or selections (opera arias by various composers, for example), and this may generate some income. Otherwise, income comes from rentals, performing rights, mechanical rights, synchronization, etc.

"We are prepared to make an investment in our search for the next Menotti or Barber. Take John Corigliano, for example; the parts and corrections for his *First Symphony* were initially extremely expensive to produce, but there have already been nearly 200 performances, plus broadcasts and two recordings. Likewise, we devoted much time and energy to *The Ghosts of Versailles* at the time of the Met performance and revival. But the success of that piece has been enormously gratifying for all of us. So the investment has paid off.

"We're increasingly interested in an exclusive relationship with our composers. Usually these are five year contracts. There are contracts which are negotiated for specific works, usually on the commercial side of the print catalog: flute music, piano music, choral octavos, etc."

What is the financial arrangement, in general?

Feder:

"The composer and publisher share royalties on print, rental, grand rights and performing rights income. The specific splits are affected by several factors: who is responsible for preparation of materials; the level of promotion put into a given work or composer; guarantees to print within a given period of time."

What materials should a composer have on hand?

Feder:

"A work list, including representative works. A good demo tape, if possible. (If you have one, make sure that it has only one piece per side. Cueing a tape doesn't work! This is very important.) A CV emphasizing history of performances so we can cross-reference, or make calls, and Various narrative bios for use in programs. A CD is good if you have one, since you can cue it easily, and the quality is usually predictable. Program notes and reviews."

To what extent do you now rely on computers for printing

Feder:

"We've put virtually all our new works on computer, from which we extract parts. This makes the rehearsals more effective and efficient because of the legibility and accuracy of performing materials, and revisions are easy to make."

What about composers self-publishing, using the computer? And working with a personal representative to oversee the business aspects of their careers?

Feder:

"It's inevitable that composers are increasingly going to use computers to copy and print their music, just as writers have gone to word processors. They will still need good editors, to ensure things like consistency, correct orthography, input on practicality and effectiveness of written choices, etc. The bookkeeping aspects of the publishing business are formidable. The licensing registration(s), fee calculation and collection, etc. are best left to professionals. Also, storage and cataloging of materials can be a major undertaking.

"But, a personal representative can work with other aspects of a composer's career: speaking and teaching engagements, performance engagements, and general publicity. We also tend to make a distinction between promotion and publicity, focusing our efforts on getting the next performance rather than the next newspaper feature."

Any final words?

Feder:

"Music publishers tread a delicate path between art and commerce, between the traditional long-term view of developing artistic potential and profile, and the new demands brought about by changing and competitive technologies and markets. It's exciting to be exploring new international arenas for contemporary music as well as new media opportunities, and we look forward to opening these up not only for our own composers but also for contemporary music in general."

Jennifer Bilfield, President, Boosey & Hawkes

How does a composer get on your roster?

Bilfield:

"Composers have found their way to Boosey & Hawkes through recommendation from colleagues and other B & H composers, personal approaches to the company, and through performances of works which have piqued our interest. [Between 1985 and 1997] we signed exclusive contracts with 12 composers: John Adams, Louis Andriessen, Harrison Birtwistle, Unsuk Chin, Henryk Gorecki, H.K. Gruber, David Home,

Magnus Lindberg, Steve Mackey, James MacMillan, Michael Torke, and Christopher Rouse."

Why do you take on so few composers?

Bilfield:

"The number of living composers in the Serious Music Division who have exclusive contracts with the company has been kept deliberately modest (26 in all) for several reasons. The first is the fact that it appears to be the most productive for all parties involved. Another stems from the fact that while many publishers have one office and are represented abroad by other publishers in an agency relationship, Boosey & Hawkes is an international company with offices in New York, London, Berlin, and Sydney. As such, each affiliate plays an active role in promoting/selling the composer's music once he or she joins our roster. The resources required to support a composer's music through such an international network are considerable, but often invisible to those outside the industry. For example, we negotiate contracts and commissions; license works for recordings, media uses and other rights; protect the copyright of works in tandem with the performing rights societies; provide editorial and production support for musical materials; field requests for biographies, program notes, reviews and photos; and coordinate promotional activity through industry contacts, conferences, concert travel, and printed materials. Composers who approach Boosey & Hawkes to enter into a publishing relationship cite these resources as principal attractions, along with the quality of communication between the affiliates and prestige of the catalog.

"In addition to the Serious Music Division, Boosey & Hawkes works with composers through its Printed Materials Division, which has recently begun to develop exclusive relationships with composers for our choral, band and educational projects.

"In short, we want to work with composers who have defined their own voice and who have a clear sense of the direction of their work and how it fits within the continuum of musical life, both past and future. If we can find music which will stay active throughout the life of the copyright, it can eventually be profitable for both the composer and company."

Is it worth sending music to a publisher?

Bilfield:

"Yes, but do approach several companies. Be sure that you know what type of music they publish and are currently considering, and why you want to work with them. Most publishers have committees that review submissions. Generally, composers are encouraged to send recordings and scores of works which represent the direction of their current writing, along with a list of performances, and forthcoming projects and performances. As mentioned above, recommendations are extremely helpful, and can often expedite the review process. I always suggest that composers add publishers to their mailing list in order to keep us apprised of upcoming performances and activities."

What is the place of print in your activities?

Bilfield:

"Each year we produce scores that are available at retail music stores. Additional scores, particularly those of very recent works, can be obtained directly from us by special order.

"Many printed scores are used to enhance promotional activities, while others such as Bartok's *Concerto for Orchestra* or John Adam's *Short Ride in a Fast Machine* have strong sales, year after year, and become staples of the repertoire."

How about computers?

Bilfield:

"Computer engraved scores are now standard, and without question are expected by most performing organizations. Many composers do have access to sophisticated systems and software, and this does help to expedite revisions and corrections. Given the limited rehearsal time available to many performers, the accuracy and clarity of score and parts is paramount, and can make the pivotal difference between a passable and excellent performance."

What materials should a composer have on hand?

Bilfield:

"A good tape or CD is the most important tool a composer has in promoting his or her music - to anyone. Well-produced scores are also useful, but will generally be reviewed only after the work has been heard; they are also much more expensive than CDs for the composers to reproduce and mail. Quantities of up-to-date reviews, performance history, program notes, and resumes are also important to have on hand to avoid last-minute scrambles for information.

"Regardless of how a piece appears on paper, it must work in performance. The recording is *(or should be)* the next best thing to being there."

What about self-publishing?

Bilfield:

"If a composer opts for this route, she or he needs to be realistic about the amount of time self-publishing entails. A part-time assistant can provide support in copying, collating, fielding calls, billing and perhaps even in publicity, so that the composer can spend his or her time composing."

Any final words?

Bilfield:

"Perhaps the two most critical elements in a composer's career are developing craft, and building a network of musicians who are passionate advocates of his or her work. Admittedly, these facets of a composer's life are often at odds. While the act of composing is solitary and all-consuming, composers write music largely to communicate, express, incite, inspire. It should go without saying that composers should make every effort to interact with performers, although many are uncomfortable promoting their music. Ultimately, music is most eloquent, most persuasive when it is heard, performed and experienced by others. Everything else is icing on the cake."

Publishers

From the composer's point of view

Composers have much more ambivalent feelings about publishers, generally, than the other way around. The frustrations they commonly express about their publishers are strikingly similar to those expressed by performers about their managers: "Their choices are arbitrary;" "They're not knowledgeable;" "They never get me commissions or performances;" "I get them myself, and split the royalties."

These days, it's perfectly possible, with a relatively small investment, to get yourself set up with a computer, printer, and the right software, and print your own music to rent or sell to those interested. Says Oliver Knussen:

> "If you are concerned about this [getting a publisher], ask yourself why, other than wanting your name in a well-known catalogue, do you want to be published? The only answer is that it is becoming a major inconvenience to deal with the demand for your work. When you do sign up, realize that you effectively lose 50% of the income from your work. Print sales royalties are negligible, but you will only get between 25% and 50% of rentals. Retainers are very unlikely anymore. Working independently, with a representative or assistant who can handle many of these aspects of your business, is a good idea. If you have stage works, or works involving text, the grand rights agreements are very complicated, probably best dealt with by a publisher, though an assistant should be able to learn how to deal with them in time."

So, just as with performers, you may well start out – and even end up – self-managing and self-publishing.

202

Self publishing, self-management and personal representatives

If you decide to go this route, you will need to learn about copying, probably using a computer and a software program like *Sibelius* or *Finale;* you will need to work very hard, as described above, on creating a market for your work by creating strong relationships with those who might commission or perform it; and you will need to be both organized and businesslike about fulfilling the administrative aspects of your compositional life.

In terms of working with a representative, know that there are very few representatives around who work with composers - and even fewer good ones. One path to explore might be to find someone with the skills and personal qualifications you feel you need, that complement your own strengths (and weaknesses): computer ability; good negotiating skills, to set commissioning and other fees; organizational ability; a good working relationship with many performers; above all, a strong, enthusiastic belief in your music. Even if this person has little or no experience in this line of work, it will be possible to train him to act on your behalf, perhaps at first principally secretarially, then increasingly as publisher, manager, or in as many roles as you are both comfortable.

Other important skills for composers:
Talking to audiences and writing program notes

The musical world into which most young composers are emerging is not one which comes equipped with a public eager for the composer's next contribution. Composers, like performers - perhaps even more than performers - must be prepared to convince others of the value of their work. More often than not, this will be accomplished through words and personality, even before the music gets heard. How an audience, or performer, or potential supporter, hears your work, will depend on the way the listener feels about you - and about new music in general, of course, and a variety of other factors as well. The first of these is, however, the only one under your immediate control, so use it.

The tips for performers on speaking directly to audiences in Chapter XI, "On-Stage," are equally applicable to composers. Assuming that you are not performing the work yourself, the period in which you speak directly to listeners is your chance to create the atmosphere or the background against which you want the work to be heard. Something personal or anecdotal is more helpful to this end than something technical. Interesting the audience in you and your music is more engaging, and will result in the audience listening with sympathy and interest, than discussions of structure. Come up with a short list of things you might say, as you will often be called upon to briefly speak if you show up at the performance. And, of course, you should always do that if you can.

Program notes are another way of speaking to an audience. They should actually achieve something in the way of enlightenment, not substitute for listening. Avoid anything like the following (these notes have been altered only very slightly from those provided at a recent composer's concert at a major music school):

> "This piece is based on principles associated with twelve tone structures but also concerns itself with the organized distribution of various levels of contrast and continuity. The rigidity of fixed interval structures did not provide internal organization for this music, but rather the mechanisms of transformation that proceed over time, the consistency between the interaction of the parts rather than the derivation of the parts themselves."

What?

This isn't useful. If the concert takes place, as this one did, in a conservatory and at a composer's concert, these notes seem to presume that only fellow composers are welcome to attend, since obviously they're the only ones who might marginally care about all that. If the piece is well written, the performance is decent and the audience is knowledgeable - as it almost certainly was in this case -the piece doesn't need this kind of annotation; one should be able to hear musical structure, generally if not specifically. If the piece isn't well written, these notes won't make it any better; if the performance isn't good, the audience won't be persuaded to make allowances because of the compelling text; if the audience isn't knowledgeable, notes like these will make them actively hostile. Notes should be a bridge to the music, and an inviting bridge at that, which at their best should make the audience want to close their programs and listen.

204

It would be best at this point if we could provide a really good example of a program note; we haven't done so, because really good ones are hard to find, and really good ones are often so specifically about a particular work that they might be off-putting, because the kind of work described isn't like the reader's. But we do have a few suggestions. First: since it's often very difficult to write notes about your own music, perhaps several composers could get together and write about each other's music. Since these notes would be written from the point of view of what someone sympathetic and informed actually hears, they would likely be in line with what the composer hopes the ideal listener will also hear, and possibly can point the listener in the right direction. Also, it's good to get into the habit of listening supportively to the music of colleagues, and this would help to create a formal way of doing this.

Another idea, that composers may be uncomfortable with, but that *every* listener we've spoken too really likes: ***state the length of the piece***. This gives the first time listener a framework within which to listen, much like going into a museum and judging where to stand depending on the size of the canvas. And it is actually "hard news," so to speak, one of the things a listener simply doesn't know beforehand. A third item, if the notes are recent, or can be updated: if the work is not a new one, how does it relate to the composer's ongoing style, and how does he feel about it now. This one could be tricky, but would certainly be interesting.

Materials

In the text above we've referred to materials that the composer needs in order to be prepared when someone asks for them, as they will. The items which are absolutely indispensable are:

A good demo CD or tape, or better several, which highlight one aspect or another of your work (see Chapter III for specific advice on this).

A repertoire list, including instrumentation, timings, and performance history (or combinations of these).

A narrative biography.

A curriculum vitae.

All should have the appropriate contact information on them, of course. See Chapter II, "Written and Visual Materials," for performers.

Additional useful items, if you can afford them or if they've somehow appeared in your musical life:

A photo, so that it can be reproduced in programs or on posters;

A CD.

A Promotional Brochure, which combines much of the above. Many publishers put these together for their roster composers, just as a manager would for performers.

Examples of a current repertoire list and narrative biography of young composer Gordon Beeferman follows.

Example 1: Narrative Biography

GORDON BEEFERMAN, composer
Address
Tel/Fax
www.gordon.inkbox.org
gordonbeeferman@inkbox.org

GORDON BEEFERMAN is becoming recognized as a unique and gifted composer. His compositions include works for piano, voice, orchestra, guitar and various chamber groups. His music has been performed in New York, Boston, Chicago, Los Angeles, Minneapolis, Rome, and elsewhere. The Chicago Tribune praised Beeferman for his "masterly orchestral craftmanship… odd, refreshing sonorities and expressive speech." The Albany Times-Union described his work as "chilling…unpredictable…brutal."

A native of Cambridge, Mass., Beeferman was born in 1976. He played piano from an early age; as a teenager he studied jazz and Third Stream with Ran Blake and Hankus Netsky of the New England Conservatory. He is a graduate of the University of Michigan School of Music, where he received his B.M. in composition and was awarded the Stanley Medal, the School's highest undergraduate honor. His teachers have included William Albright, William Bolcom and Leslie Bassett.

Beeferman has received much recognition for his work, including three BMI Student Composer Awards (including the 2002 William Schuman prize), an ASCAP Young Composer Award, and the BMG/Williams College National Awards to Young Composers Grand Prize. He has been a fellow at Tanglewood (2001) and a resident composer at the Copland House (2000). He has received grants from the American Music Center and has been commissioned by the New York Youth Symphony, guitarist David Leisner, the Albany Symphony Orchestra, Concert Artists Guild and Premiere Commission, Inc.

A "fully liberated pianist" (Cadence Magazine), Beeferman moves easily across the boundaries between composition, interpretation and improvisation. He has performed in a wide range of settings, from concerto soloist to free-improviser, and collaborated with both writers and dancers. Recently he has performed at the Merce Cunningham Studio, Music at the Anthology (NYC), the Improvised and Otherwise Festival (Brooklyn), the Zeitgeist Gallery (Cambridge), and the San Francisco Alternative Music Festival. He and percussionist Jeff Arnal have released a CD of new improvised music, Bodies of Water, on Generate Records.

Beeferman lives and works in New York City.

Example 2: Curriculum Vitae

GORDON BEEFERMAN
composer and pianist
Address
Tel/Fax
gordonbeeferman@inkbox.org
www.gordon.inkbox.org

Education:
B.M. in Composition with highest honors, University of Michigan School of Music, 1998
    (Composition studies with William Albright, William Bolcom, Leslie Bassett; piano studies with Anton Nel)
Private studies in jazz and Third Stream at the New England Conservatory
    with Ran Blake & Hankus Netsky, 1989-92

Honors, Awards, Commissions, and Fellowships:
Commissions from the Albany Symphony Orchestra and Concert Artists Guild, 2002
BMI Student Composer Award, William Schuman Prize (for *San Francisco Songs*), 2002
American Music Center / Jory Copying Grant, 2002
Tanglewood Music Center, composition fellow, 2001
Copland Heritage Association composer residency, 2000
American Music Center / Jory Copying Grant, 1999
Civic Orchestra of Chicago First Hearing winner, 1999
BMI Student Composer Award, 1998 (*Symphony #1*)
FIRST MUSIC commission (*Piano Quartet*), New York Youth Symphony Chamber Music Program, 1998
Stanley Medal, University of Michigan School of Music, 1998 (highest award to a graduating senior)
ASCAP/Morton Gould Awards to Young Composers, 1997 (*Sonata Bombastica*)
BMG/Williams College National Young Composers Award, Grand Prize, College
    Chamber Music category, 1997
Winner, University of Michigan Concerto Performance Competition, 1996-97
BMI Student Composer Award, 1996 (*Now No One Will Listen to Songs*)

Selected recent performances of compositions:
Morbidity and Mortality Report premiered by the Albany Symphony Orchestra, March 2003
Symphony #1 (mvts. 1 and 2) read by Minnesota Orchestra at their March 2002 reading sessions
Safe, This Dangerous Night at Jordan Hall, Boston MA (premiere, Dec. 2000), David Leisner, guitar
San Francisco Songs (for tenor and piano) at Greenwich House Music School, NYC, March 2001,
    and Tanglewood Festival of Contemporary Music, Aug. 2001
Piano Quartet at Weill Recital Hall, New York, April 1999
    (premiere, New York Youth Symphony chamber players)
La Aurora (from Symphony #1) at Orchestra Hall, Chicago (Civic Orchestra of Chicago, premiere, April 1999)

Selected performances as pianist:
Duo of new improvised music with percussionist Jeff Arnal, performances at the Knitting Factory, NYC;
    Zeitgeist Gallery, Cambridge, Mass.; Tremont Theater, Boston, Mass.; Improvised and Otherwise Festival,
    Brooklyn, NY; Music at the Anthology, NYC; San Francisco Alternative Music Festival
Performance of own compositions at Greenwich House Music School, New York City, March 2001

Recordings:
"Bodies of Water," with percussionist Jeff Arnal, released Dec.2001 on Generate Records

Other:
Co-founder of "Caterwaul," a new music/theater ensemble in Ann Arbor, Mich., 1998

Example 3: Repertoire list

GORDON BEEFERMAN
Works

2003:   **City Shore**
Dance score for solo piano
Written for Anita Cheng Dance
Premiere January 9-10-11, 2003, at the Merce Cunningham Studio, New York.

2002:   **Morbidity and Mortality Report**
For full orchestra
Commissioned by the BMI Foundation / Carlos Surinach Fund for David Alan Miller and
the Albany Symphony Orchestra
Premiere March 14, 2003 at the Troy Savings Bank Hall, Troy, NY

Phenomena
For solo piano
Commissioned by Linda and Jack Hoeschler for Concert Artists Guild and written for
Alpin Hong, with additional support from Premiere Commission, Inc.

2000:   **Safe, This Dangerous Night**
for solo guitar
Commissioned by guitarist David Leisner
Premiered by Leisner November 29, 2000 at Jordan Hall, Boston. Further performances
by Leisner: March 10, 2001 at the Greenwich House Music School, New York; May
18, 2001 at the 19th International Guitar Festival, Milan, Italy; May 21, 2001 at
Fondazione Arts Academy, Rome, Italy

San Francisco Songs
for tenor and full orchestra. also version for piano
Premiered by Tony Boutté, tenor, and Gordon Beeferman, piano, at Greenwich House
Music School, March 10, 2001. Excerpts performed at the Tanglewood Festival of
Contemporary Music, August 10, 2001.

1998:   **Piano Quartet**
for piano, violin, viola, and cello
Premiered at Weill Recital Hall at Carnegie Hall, New York, April 7, 1999 by members
of the NY Youth Symphony Chamber Music Program. Second performance at the
Greenwich House Music School, March 10, 2001

The Greek Gaze
"mini-opera" for 3 women, 2 men, electric guitar, electric bass, and drums
Premiered by "Caterwaul" at the University of Michigan, March 27, 1998.

Page 1

1998:   **Sesame Street Variations**
        for piano solo, based on themes from the television series "Sesame Street"
        Premiered by Gordon Beeferman at the University of Michigan, April 26, 1998

1997:   **Symphony #1**
        for full orchestra
        Winner of 1998 BMI Student Composer Award.
        Third movement, "La Aurora (The Dawn In New York)" premiered by the Civic
            Orchestra of Chicago at Orchestra Hall, Chicago, April 11, 1999; second performance
            by the Young Musicians Foundation Debut Orchestra, Wilshire Ebell Theater, Los
            Angeles, May 16, 1999.

1996:   **Sonata Bombastica**
        for violin and piano
        Winner of BMG/Williams College National Young Composers Award
            and ASCAP Award.
        Premiered February 10, 1997 at the University of Michigan by violinist Gabriel Bolkosky
            and Gordon Beeferman at the piano. Second performance at Berkshire New Music
            Festival, Williamstown, Mass. Third performance at Weill Recital Hall, New York
            City, January 19, 1999 by Doris Stevenson and Maria Bachmann. Further
            performances: May 24, 2001 at New York University's Loeb Theater by Composers
            Concordance.

        Three Night Moods
        for two harps and two percussion
        Premiered April 14, 1997 at the University of Michigan. Version for two pianos and
            percussion premiered July 17, 1996 at the Gamper Festival of Contemporary Music.

1995:   **Now No One Will Listen To Songs**
        for bass-baritone, B-flat clarinet, violin, cello, and piano; settings of Russian texts by
            Akhmatova, Bobyshev, Lermontov, and Mandelstam
        Winner of BMI Student Composer Award.
        First complete performance by Collage New Music with bass-baritone David Ripley, at
            the C. Walsh Theater in Boston, Mass., March 31, 1996.

1994:   **Anonymous Lyrics**
        for soprano and piano, settings of anonymous ancient Greek texts translated by
            Richmond Lattimore
        Premiered September 15, 1996 at the Society for New Music, Syracuse, NY, by soprano
            Jane Rodgers and pianist Kevin Bylsm

X. Fine tuning

The following are thoughts and commentary about issues specific to singers, some advice to pianists, and a few words about teaching and performing, questions about which consistently arise in our discussions about the profession.

For Singers

The world sometimes seems to be a particularly rough place for singers. There are a great many of you, and the market - yes, even for tenors - is extraordinarily competitive. As in any part of the business, there are opportunities, and quality, determination, collegiality, imagination and professionalism will find and make the most of them. But, it's tough.

So, what follows is advice and ideas aimed specifically at singers, with headings as to general subject matter, followed by a few hopefully helpful tips. Though we haven't cited the sources (there are too many of them), they include singers, managers and others knowledgeable about the vocal world.

The patience factor. The first thing to remember, which is both discouraging and reassuring, is that it takes time to build a vocal career. Lots of time. One friend of ours in the vocal world suggests that it takes eight years to see if anything will happen, and another five to stabilize whatever has happened. Perhaps this doesn't sound too bad, until you measure your progress, if you're unwise enough to do this against other people - perhaps non-musicians - who graduated from college when you did, and who after thirteen years are dealing with mid-career success, not thinking about whether to stick it out or learn computer programming. A manager we know described the career of one of his quite successful singers, one which has a very happy ending, who took sixteen years to go from small opera engagements to quite regular work at the Met. Again, this may not sound too long until you think about all the years after getting out of school, before he had those first small-ish opera roles, and before he had a manager hustling the better auditions. Modestly, add another five to ten.

Beyond *la bella voce*. Because the time frame is usually so long, you will have to find ways to survive in the meantime, as well as ways to honestly assess how you're doing. (This is certainly not a problem unique to singers, but the trajectory is flatter, the speed slower, in-the-field ways of getting by more scarce, and objective feedback perhaps more difficult to come by.) You may be able to slant things slightly more to your advantage, at least as far as getting some consistent work is concerned, if you have a specific interest or ability that you can be identified with: early music, new music, certain types of opera roles. Working with composers can be particularly helpful for singers: there's some work to be had, as well as opportunities for musical growth and being part of the creative process. There also are chances to get to know instrumentalists, as much new vocal music is for chamber ensemble rather than voice and piano; since singers are often somewhat isolated from the rest of the music community, this can be a very important way of meeting and working with your fellow musicians. Additionally, the better trained you are as a musician, and the more skills you develop, the more likely it is that you'll be able to take advantage of opportunities that arise and create opportunities for yourself.

Europe or bust? Given how hard it is to make a dent in the profession, at this point, the question arises as to whether to try to build a career first (that is, an opera career) in Europe. There certainly are things to be said in favor of this, though it's not the absolute requirement that it once was. Many managers like singers who've spent some time on stages in Europe, as they return with language skills, contacts, and experience. And there is work in Europe, in part because local training is very good. But sometimes coming home is hard; for several artists we know who want to sing in the U.S. and make their lives here, being out of the loop too long without local exposure can make it very difficult to return.

Management. Do you absolutely need a manager? No. Can you function without one? Yes. Can you make a serious, notable career? Ultimately, no. You can work, and you can, with a great deal of hustle, keep track of audition possibilities, particularly if you coach with someone who knows who's in town and whose schedule is what, and if you're a good networker with lots of friends looking for the same auditions. As in other parts of the business, some sponsors actually prefer not to deal with managers, and others are willing to work without them. But, most opera companies, and certainly all the major ones won't audition artists not under management, and at some point, you will need it.

But, in some ways, it may be easier (not easy, but easier) for a singer to find a manager than for an instrumentalist, for two reasons. First, because there are lots of managements, really booking agencies, specifically for singers: in fact, several non-specialized managers we know prefer to work with singers who have already been with a "singers" management first. And second, because above all managers are looking for beautiful voices, and if they fall in love with yours, that can balance out all sorts of other factors. Sometimes the factor which makes all the difference is the good overall musicianship, as noted above. The three sopranos on one management's very prestigious roster all started off playing the violin, and only came to voice later as a profession. Their good, solid musical skills and background, in addition to their vocal ability, made them more versatile, far easier to place, and therefore much more appealing to the management.

Money. A brief aside about the financial arrangements between management and singers: Commissions may be about 20% for concert fees, 10% for opera fees, but it can get very complicated; management may take a fee from gross or not; sometimes the fee is calculated on a per performance basis; and overall, which elements of the contract are subject to commission are variable. Sorry, it's not consistent. You will need to be prepared for almost anything. And the money may not be great, even for good jobs. An oratorio engagement which took place a few seasons ago, with a major orchestra got $1,500 + air fare for the young, not unknown singer they hired; the same singer received $1,000 + hotel for two Messiahs with a regional orchestra in the south. Most opera engagements underpay as well, perhaps $1,500-$2,500 per performance for mid-range companies, perhaps with transportation, perhaps with a per diem or a guest room in someone's home. One regional company paid $5,000, + $750 per show, for 6 weeks, plus air fare and housing; the manager took 10%.

Other vocal work. What other work, outside of simply temping, is there while you're working hard to develop your voice and credentials, get some exposure, and network? There is paid choral work, though it's scarce. Churches and synagogues pay very badly, generally around $70 to $85 a Sunday with one rehearsal (tenors get more): but you can meet conductors, other singers, and learn about opportunities from them. (Vocal contractors names are usually common knowledge; good sight reading is absolutely necessary. Let your friends know you can sub.) Teaching may be a good option, if you can find some steady situation, and if you're good at it. There is some commercial work, but there are very few commercials though that want a classical sound. But if you're in New York, you can go to SAG (the Screen Artists Guild) and check the boards, and keep talking to people.

And if you're in New York or another city with an active theater community, you may be able to get work in the musical theater. Know that this is still something done with varying success and very mixed reviews. Aside from the musical demands of each area, the classical field is still fairly snobbish about artists who have made their reputations doing what is considered to be commercial or pop work. But it's not impossible to cross from one to the other, as long as you keep all these factors in mind, and there's certainly great music, as well as perhaps a living, to be had by being proficient on both sides of this musical divide.

Weight. Questions about this come up frequently at our workshops, so we thought we should at least mention it. Our various experts have noted that large people need to understand that if a director has a choice between two singers, equally good, if one is noticeably too fat they will choose the other. It sounds obvious, but the question is asked, and therefore deserves a straight answer. Everyone needs to keep in shape, exercise, breathe, take care of themselves, and understand that there may be situations in which someone will lose out for only this reason.

Hints about auditions. As always, find out as much as you can about the situation and what will be expected of you so that you can wear the right clothes, and sing the right things. What you do should fit the call, musically. For opera auditions, the first aria should be what you can sing when you roll out of bed; you must own it. Then be ready with something else, preferably four other things. Don't give the auditioner(s) a hard time, and remember that collegiality is <u>really</u> important. Don't concern yourself with the reaction of the moment. One friend did an audition in which the listeners talked through the entire audition, but he got the job; they later told him that they were discussing where they could use him.

Another singer friend heard about auditions for the Met chorus on the day they were taking place, because he was riding home on the bus with someone who was auditioning. He walked in, auditioned, and got about $20,000 in work for the next season. Moral: be musically prepared at all times and always carry a resume and picture with you.

Assorted tips: take the ones you like.

Find a teacher whose students are working.

Get out of school. This doesn't mean that you shouldn't be well-educated, but rather that too many singers substitute another degree for the risks of the professional world. You can survive: there are day jobs to help you get by, and there are study grants and apprenticeship programs.

Understand that there are some people who simply won't take to your voice.

Learn to network! It's a very social business. Opportunities resulting from cancellations start with emergency phone calls to colleagues and friends.

You probably need to go to New York at some point, but are you aware of the cost? Coaches, teachers, etc. are expensive. Come to New York with some saleable skills, and when you're ready.

Sing everything and go anywhere, if it's fun.

Pianists: Work after graduation

A few pointers, very briefly. Pianists, like singers, often seem isolated in the musical community without the easy camaraderie of the orchestra player and the resulting connection to work opportunities. But pianists have advantages in the field, among them:

- All those violinists, instrumentalists and singers need your services, and that means that there will be work for you if you're prepared for it

- The fact that pianists are absolutely necessary for so many musical situations – from dance classes to local theater presentations

- The fact that the piano is a popular instrument, that it has such an enormous and strong repertoire, and that so many people want to take piano lessons

- The fact that having learned the piano (reading scores rather than parts, for example) gives you a basis for going in many directions - conducting, coaching, accompaniment, free-lancing, teaching, and more.

You also have disadvantages in addition to the isolation mentioned above, among them:

- Situations in which there is no piano available

- That enormous and strong repertoire, which sometimes results in less creativity in finding a niche, and pressure to achieve an extraordinarily high standard of performance in the standard literature which limits the time needed to explore.

A pianist needs, in thinking about her goals, to consider what skills and credentials will be helpful in achieving them.

If you improvise, sight read, score read, or transpose, know the literature for a particular instrument or instruments, can communicate verbally, play electronic keyboards (for orchestral as well as commercial opportunities), handle music others can't, read figured bass, play harpsichord, read unusual notation, and play complex contemporary music, etc. or some combination of these, you can possibly work (in no particular order) as a repitateur in an opera house; as a singers' coach, or an instrumental accompanist; as a member of a chamber ensemble, new music ensemble or early music group; perform concerts which include conversation or lectures as part of the format; in commercial music; to name only a very few.

The above assumes that, even if your goal is to be a solo pianist performing standard repertoire, you need to keep busy, keep eating, and keep your name and presence out there, along the way. Since pianists may, after graduating, find the phone even more silent than their non-pianist colleagues do, think about starting your own project: forming a group, developing a special concert or in-school performance, and finding venues for it (see "Self-management"); developing a concept for a radio series, finding the funding, and bringing it to the local college or public station. What should guide you, when deciding whether to start or even take on a project, is: *If I Do This, Will I Learn Something?* If the answer is yes, do it.

Teaching and Performing

A pianist friend of ours, who teaches at a major music conservatory, was discussing his life and career. Someone to be reckoned with during his own conservatory days, he now, in addition to his teaching, performs at some music festivals (not the most high-profile ones) on a regular basis, does the occasional recording, and performs a few concerts each year. His students are gifted, and he makes a respectable living. He's not famous, but he's known in the profession, and respected. And yet he's slightly bitter, and certainly feels that he should have had more.

However, a major performing career *during the building stage* probably can't co-exist comfortably with a major teaching position. Balancing the demands of teaching - which requires lots of time for planning, being consistently, or at least predictably, available to students, staying in one place, and focusing on the requirements of others - with the demands of building a life in solo or chamber performance on a standard solo instrument - which requires being ready for anything, traveling, intensive networking and focusing to some degree on one's own musical vision - is not realistic. Our friend made a choice, and is, sadly, not comfortable with its consequences.

This is not to say that one can't both teach and perform, and do them successfully and contentedly -if your definition of success includes the kind of activity our friend finds too limited. Obviously it can be done, and it is done, all the time. And certainly senior artists, who have the stature which allows them, without risk, to set limits on either their performing or teaching as necessary, are in the enviable position of being able to have their cake and eat it too.

However, let's turn this around for a minute, and assume that the life described in the first paragraph of this section is exactly what the reader aspires to. In this case, in today's academic climate it is very much to the aspiring teacher's advantage to have significant performing credentials, often more negotiable than another degree (unless, of course, the position requires particular scholarly expertise).

Academic positions at fine music schools, more often than not, depend on the candidate's having a significant professional performing life. Such professional involvement allows the teacher to provide first hand musical knowledge and experience to their students, but also to provide the institution with connections to power and quality in the field, essential for attracting the best performing students. The better the school, the more of these kinds of connections it needs from its teachers and provides to its students. So, in this sense, balancing the two helps to get you a teaching job. It rarely works the other way around, and we have never heard of a case where an academic appointment helped to get a major performing career up and running.

Balancing both, then, requires some perspective and self-knowledge. At the same time, it requires an ability to keep motivated about your performing career; it can be all too easy to trade off the more predictable demands of the academic life, and its relative security, for the hustling one must do to stay performing. Some artists we know have postponed taking or even applying for teaching jobs until their forties, or fifties, or whenever their careers were reasonably secure (or clearly not going to go much further anyway), to insure that they didn't loose the "edge" they need to keep them in the trenches. For "edge," read not knowing where the rent is coming from, fear of having to go into another field, and just plain ambition - which can be a useful, in fact probably essential, part of getting a major career going.

A teaching job, though, can become the center of your performing life, and can allow you to become the central figure in a number of entrepreneurial projects, including establishing a concert series and hiring artists to perform in it, or forming ensembles with your colleagues and performing both at your home base and on tour. So, a teaching position can in some cases enhance, rather than limit, your options. If you do want the option of finding an academic position at some point, you can be more hirable if you develop

- Visibility in the field
- A broad range of interests
- A reputation as a teacher of master classes
- A specialty, or special relationships in the field, scholarly or otherwise.

This will all help you to attract students, which is key as far as the institution is concerned, as well as to be a good teacher. From the students' point of view, they are seeking a teacher who is inspiring, truly involved with discovering the artistic truth within each student; who has prestige, and/or power (these are different, or can be); and who can get them work, and help them to be competitive in today's world. By keeping active in both worlds, your chances of providing all of these are greatly enhanced.

A final word about teaching, what we believe a fine and an honest teacher owes to their students, and what a performing teacher is especially qualified to provide:

- Your special knowledge of and experiences in the field.
- Curiosity about the repertoire, and feedback to them as to where you believe their musical strengths lie.
- An understanding of the collegial nature of the business, and encouragement of their making alliances with other musicians.
- Emphasis on versatility as well as on skills.
- Discussion of goals. Realizing the teacher's ongoing responsibility to ask, "What will you do?" and "How can I help?"

IX. On Stage

When CAG presented its Career Moves *workshops, we often opened them with a session on stage technique with the stage director and coach Janet Bookspan presiding. We started with this session because it was exciting and physically involving, but also because it went right to the heart of one of the workshops' most important issues: that, no matter how well you play, it is possible to <u>prevent</u> your music from reaching others by not realizing that your audience is experiencing more than just the notes. We relied on Janet Bookspan to bring out the best each artist had to offer, with great kindness, insight, and acuity.*

If we agree that the essence of successful musical performance is successful communication, we will agree that, just as it's hard to have a sensible telephone conversation on a line filled with static, it's hard for a listener to hear what you have to communicate when confronted with distractions that detract from the total experience. We've all attended concerts which we've liked a lot less than we might have because of factors not in the performer's control: the hall has been cold, the seats have been hard, the people next to us wouldn't stop unwrapping candy. Sometimes we've been able to overlook these factors, and sometimes not. Equally, if you, the performer, fail in those areas which are under your control to make your audience comfortable and confident, to include them in your musical vision rather than separate them from it, you've given yourself an additional handicap in trying to communicate with them that you may not be able to overcome.

True, some artists can transcend this problem, and we all know of cases where artists who are clearly ill-at-ease on stage become magical, once they start to play and we close our eyes. But not very many: most artists whom we enjoy going to hear put us at ease immediately, make us feel that there are great things coming, and, above all, shrink the space psychologically between the listener and the performer to almost nothing, so that we can - for a moment perhaps - see the world, musically, through another's eyes.

Specifically, this means being aware that you have a physical presence on stage which is noted by your audience, and that it is your responsibility to clear away the static, the physical debris, which comes between you and the audience's ability to hear your music. It also means that, to push the telephone analogy a bit further, that you must avoid "crossed wires". Just as your listener can't focus on what you have to say while hearing someone else's conflicting conversation, you have to be sure that you're not projecting two different messages in your performance, one in your music and the other in everything else you do on stage.

Usually, an audience will feel what you **seem** to be feeling (as distinct from what you actually are feeling), whether that is confident, relaxed, excited - or quite the opposite of these. You will have to see yourself as others do - a very, very difficult task. It also means that you may have to tackle, from time to time, outdated concert conventions, and take an active part in changing them.

We cannot touch here on any but the most general considerations about stage performance style. It is impossible to make rules like, "Smile"; "Always count to three before turning away from the audience"; "Wear velvet"; "Don't wear velvet"; "Move, and be expressive"; "Stop moving, and be less distracting." Though there are general ways of dealing with specific stage problems, this degree of personal specificity is silly, because what you do on stage must come out of the same truth which informs who and what you are as a musician. In developing your performance technique on your instrument, for example, you learn to play cleanly and accurately, usually through a set course of scales, exercises and etudes so that you can project the overall line and structure and not have it sound like a jumble. But the *reason you* want to be able to project line and structure, in the end, is so that you can project *your vision* of the line and the structure, which is not anyone else's. Similarly, developing your on-stage technique is, first, a matter of developing a smoothness of presentation which clears away any distractions which come between you and your listeners; and, second, developing an on-stage technique which is, part of your total communication, which enables you to be most effective at communicating your ideas.

Even the most generally applicable rules regarding performance presentation technique need hands-on work, or a very lengthy discussion beyond the scope of this chapter, or both. Therefore, our specific recommendations will be limited to directing your attention to potential trouble spots, and stating, at the end of the section, one general consideration which will inform your approach to being on stage.

First: think about *all* aspects of your performance, including the non-playing ones.

Just thinking about how you are going to get on and off stage, how long and whether to bow before you start and where you should look when you receive applause after you play, whom you should acknowledge and how, where you will put a handkerchief, what you're wearing, and on and on, puts you very far ahead of most emerging performers (and a whole lot of experienced ones), who just plunge on stage and hope for the best.

In thinking about these issues, watch other performers carefully. Pay attention to which performers have a performance style that seems to you to be comfortable, elegant, casual, or not distracting - whatever you admire. Watch your peers perform, and think about who seems to carry things off successfully, and who instead makes the audience confused (they may not be able to tell when the pieces end, or whether and when to applaud, for example); who projects "school recital" rather than "professional performance;" who makes everyone tense, rather than expectant, by showing a contagious lack of confidence - and what might be done to improve things.

Ask people about your stage manner

How would you describe yourself as feeling on stage, and how does that tally with how you appear to others? It's very important to see where the two views diverge, if they do, and to analyze what's creating the difference. Sometimes a very small change in one aspect of your presentation will completely alter your audience's perception, and make you more confident in the bargain.

If what you're feeling, simply, is terrified, it's probably because you're focused on the wrong aspects of what's to come or what's happened; you'll probably have to work on concentrating on positive aspects of your performance. No audience can listen positively to a performer who's obviously scared out of his wits, someone - to be more specific - who's tripped over the piano bench in getting on, fails to take a bow, never looks at the audience at all, and hides behind the music stand. See the end of this chapter for a bit more advice regarding dealing with fear, but also know that the more you have all aspects of your performance under some kind of control, the more confident and the less fearful you will be.

Look at physical mannerisms which may be getting in your way

In these days of comparatively cheap video recorders, everyone can find someone who has one (perhaps your school videotapes performances, or could), and every performer should, at some early point, tape and watch herself perform. It may be unsettling at first, so never watch yourself directly following a performance or right before another. Prepare yourself with an arsenal of self-forgiving comments beforehand, reassuring yourself that you've certainly seen worse than what's to come, and that the audience seemed to like you so it couldn't have been as bad as you'll probably think it is, and that no one likes the way he looks on film at first anyway. And then watch, seriously and objectively. Get friends to watch with you, those who can be objective and honest when necessary, while remaining supportive.

Analyze what you see, and don't expect to change everything that you're less than satisfied with right away. Pick one or two of the most important areas to work on first - perhaps you are particularly awkward about how to get away from the piano between pieces, or how to acknowledge your accompanist. If a problem seems to be more general, an overall body tension which is getting in the way throughout, it almost certainly is affecting your performance as well, and should be dealt with without delay. There are lots of techniques that deal with tension problems for performers, and you should be able to work with someone individually or in a class on these issues.

Check whether you're reviewing your own concert for your audience while it's happening. And stop doing it!

Inexperienced performers often will send special bulletins to the audience, via grimaces, gestures or, occasionally, expletives, letting them know that they've played wrong notes, or not phrased perfectly, or whatever. This is no favor to the listeners, who might have been foolish enough to have been enjoying themselves up to that point, and certainly no favor to the player. Interestingly, the habit is probably exacerbated by long years at music school; by making faces every time you make a mistake, you're acknowledging errors and apologizing for them before your teachers, colleagues and other knowledgeable types have a chance to criticize - thereby proving that you may be incompetent, but you're not an idiot. Realize, therefore, that the concert hall is not the schoolroom. You're expected here to be professional, and if that means providing some of the kind of professional wizardry which makes great concerts even in the face of some wrong notes, so be it.

If concert conventions are getting between you and your audience, think about changing them

One of the biggest, and easiest to cure, obstacles coming between an audience and a performer is a music stand. It is very important, obviously, that a performer feel confident, and if having the music there on a discreetly low and to-the-side stand will prevent panic, fine; but a music stand which you use as protective fortification between you and your audience is a no-no, as is any positioning of the stand - or of yourself - which prevents effective communication.

Even concert dress can and should be tailored to put both you and your audience in the right frame of mind. When CAG recently considered what the dress would be for a series of performances in a rather remote, rural location that doesn't get many live concerts, we thought that really informal clothes would suit the location best. But we were wrong; in the end, we decided on formal dress. This community felt that the performance was a great occasion for them, and they wanted to dress up for the concert - and to be dressed up for it. In another situation – a concert for kids, for example – a young performer might more easily get the sympathetic attention of her audience if she wears jeans.

The starting time of a performance, if it's under your control, might affect how your concert is received by its audience. So might the length of the program, or the order, or whether or not you include an intermission - or three intermissions. It should all be negotiable in the best of all possible worlds, all with the aim of engaging your listeners as positively as possible.

If you have a chamber group, discuss all aspects of your performance together, in detail

Most of the very basic problems seen with soloists are even worse with chamber ensembles, who literally and regularly bump into each other getting on and off stage. All aspects of entrances, exits, bows, dress and even seating should be considered by the group; none are insignificant, and none are so sacred (or "traditional") that they can't be worked on and changed, if necessary.

Learn how to talk to your audience

Most performers are never trained to speak directly to their audiences - and yet this is a skill which is increasingly required of them. Learning how to do this is a lot easier than learning how to play, so that's part of the good news. Another good part is that if you've spoken to the audience, you often will feel barriers breaking down which will help with possible performance nerves, and allow you to play better. The bad news is that this is a skill which does have to be learned, and many people who are terrific performers on their instruments aren't naturally gifted as speakers.

If you find that you can't effectively wing it, here's a technique which will help. Make a list before the performance of several ideas which you feel will interest an audience and which will illuminate some aspect of your performance: the work, your relationship to it, your relationship to this composer, etc. You don't need more than three or four thoughts, but half of them should be personal rather than historical.

An example: a young clarinetist, performing the same program at two CAG concerts recently, introduced performances of the Brahms Trio with the identical speech - with one exception. Before one performance, he remarked on how both Mozart and Brahms had had close friends who were clarinetists, resulting in a significant body of work for this instrument from both composers. The audience listened politely. Before the other performance, he added that he was personally very grateful that those clarinetists had been such friendly guys, because not only did he have something to play, but he would never have been invited to this very nice part of the world to play this job without them. On this occasion, the audience laughed, everyone relaxed, and he had them in the palm of his hand for the performance. They listened with greater attention because they were listening to someone they felt they knew, a little.

Anything about the performance to follow is fair game, even how you learned a difficult work, or whether you loved it immediately or grew into it. Speak briefly rather than at length, certainly at first when you're learning how to do this, but look at the audience and smile at them; you're inviting them to join you in what you feel will be an enjoyable experience, and you're using this opportunity to direct their attention to some of those aspects which are most meaningful for you.

One important idea which is well worth keeping in mind is that of *sharing,* a concept which goes back to the first chapter in which you were encouraged to find out what distinguishes you as an artist. When you know what you have that's special, and what it is that you want to communicate in a specific performance, you can stop worrying quite so much about *performing or auditioning* and focus on *sharing*: that is, on including your listeners in your musical thought.

Since sharing isn't quite as scary as performing or auditioning, by employing this concept things should improve all around, both for you and for your listeners. There is a lot of perfectly good advice around about concert terrors, ranging from the "lose your fear through repeated experience" philosophy, to some quite reasonable books on the subject, to the use of medication. The sharing concept can probably help immediately, however (unlike waiting until you've performed dozens of programs), and is certainly less potentially problematical than the pharmaceutical approach.

If at some point you find that your own ability to improve your effectiveness on stage is limited, you might think about working with a professional in this field. A few sessions can make an immense difference, and may give you the confidence you need for your total performance - freeing you to concentrate on the music, which is what all this is about.

X. Summing Up

This chapter provides information on how to fit all of the above into the framework of your own musical and career growth, with particular attention to the musician still in school. It includes two subjects which didn't fit in before, but which deserve some serious attention. The first of these is about you, and your relationship to your future; the second is about all of us, and all of our futures.

It's Never Too Early To ...
A check list for the younger musician.

The very young artist doesn't need to (and probably shouldn't) try to do everything suggested for career development in the previous chapters. There are those few in the fast lane of course, for whom a great deal is generally done to push their careers forward, almost always by others: parents, teachers, managers, publicists. However, for capable, reasonably ambitious, professionally oriented younger musicians ("younger" meaning prior to emerging from the last of their formal training), here is a checklist of things which can't hurt, and almost certainly will help, to positively prepare for the future.

Get your biography and resume on a computer disk, and update the information regularly. It's good to have this information handy and available, whether it's for the hometown paper or for submitting to a competition.

Get your performances recorded. Having good examples of your most recent playing (or your most recent piece) is very important, and since you may change dramatically with each performance when you're young, get into the habit of recording everything. It's also very important to have the opportunity to review your work for yourself, and use these performances to guide your musical direction. Even a tape made from the audience by a friend you've asked to turn the machine on and off is better than nothing - and sometimes, surprisingly, can be perfectly usable.

Develop related skills and flexibility. Very few musicians do only one thing anymore; versatility can make the difference between frustration and excitement when you're in the early stages of your career, and employment or lack of same when you're further along. Related skills might include doubling on a second instrument; the ability to improvise, and certainly the ability to sight read well;

familiarity with electronic keyboards or other instruments; knowledge of early music and performance practice; knowledge of and devotion to the works of some contemporary composers. Less obviously, speaking another language may add possible performance locales to your "places to contact" list. Some administrative experience with an arts organization might help you to organize your own concert series, or to raise the funds for it - or, at least, to find a day job in an arts related area.

Develop originality in programming. While your teachers and your school are probably going to stress your mastery of the same literature everyone else knows, played in roughly the same program order and in roughly the same format, your own curiosity and interest in reaching out to your audiences should lead you to explore beyond this. When you fully emerge into the professional arena, you will have played your standard graduation recital - the one with the baroque work, the classic and/or romantic work, and the newer work, about one hours-worth played chronologically - for the last time, hopefully. The world has heard it from everyone else, including everyone famous, and has little interest in hearing you do it again. You could both shake things up a little, have much more fun, and get some attention, by playing something different, perhaps in a different order or format. But it may be up to you to explore what's out there; get in the habit of going to other people's concerts and spending some time in the music library.

Develop on-stage skills. This is addressed in the previous chapter, but it's worth thinking about early on.

Start a mailing list, starting with fans and past sponsors. There are people in your address book, including friends, relatives, contest organizers, your dentist, your travel agent, and eventually presenters, ticket buyers and industry professionals, who want to be kept up to date about your activities. The easiest way to do this is to keep this information on a computer database, so that you can update it on an ongoing basis. I'm not a fan of the annual "Dear Everyone I've Ever Known" letter, but I think that people do appreciate the occasional post card when you're on tour or at a summer festival, or a brief note (hand written or at least hand signed) or email, when you've accomplished something special.

Look out for the right competitions and performing opportunities. Keep a close eye on the school bulletin boards, and hang around the placement office. You need chances to try out what you're learning, and perhaps to earn some money along the way. Also, make sure that your teachers and other mentors know that you would like to hear about opportunities that come their way; often, such information is only passed on to the person who most recently reminded them to do so.

Start to build relationships with other musicians. This sounds absolutely obvious, but it's worth stating, since some musicians - notably composers, singers and pianists - tend to work in isolation more than others, and since even players of orchestral instruments may find themselves with a fairly musically limited circle of musical acquaintances: the students in their teacher's studio, for example. Most of the successful (meaning pretty continuously working) musicians we know still get much of their work, and even musical ideas, from the strong relationships formed while they were students. The broader these relationships the more interesting your musical life can be. Performers should be actively seeking out composers whose work they enjoy; singers should read chamber music with instrumentalists, and vice versa; pianists should do as much accompanying as they can reasonably fit in, in many disciplines. (How else can a pianist really learn to play Schubert, but by working with singers, for example? And then, there is always the accompanying work that may pay the rent ... .) It's important to periodically move out of the musical surroundings of your own school into another place, where you can come into contact with a new set of musicians and musical ideas. Summer festivals may be an ideal venue where you can broaden your artistic horizons, and there are as many different kinds of these as there are different kinds of musicians.

Most important, earlier I've mentioned getting into the habit of going to other people's concerts. It's all too common while in school to find that your time doesn't allow you to go to any but the most essential - perhaps required -events. Make the time: this is an essential part of your education as a student, a responsibility as a good colleague, and a potential delight as an artist interested in learning more about repertoire and your fellow musicians. Also, who will attend your concerts, if you don't attend those of others?.

Become knowledgeable about your field. Read the newspapers: the "think" pieces, not just the reviews. Read the specialty magazines, like *Chamber Music,* or *American Record Guide,* or your instrument specific publications. You will find out about your discipline, your colleagues, about the musical environment, and about how you can contribute as well as what opportunities there are for you.

What not to leave school without

Many musicians find themselves in post-graduation befuddlement, wondering what all those years, and many thousands of dollars, amount to, in the face of an uncertain future and very difficult job market. Rather than confront this for the first time as one is about to leave the academy, it's useful to think, upon entering it, what you don't want to leave without. My own list would include at least four items, the first of which is absolutely obvious:

A great education. You should emerge from music school with the musical and technical skills (both on and off your instrument), historical perspective and breadth of knowledge of the repertoire, to allow you to hold your own with the best young artists out there. It is clear that the degrees that you acquire will be very important (sometimes essential) if your future plans include teaching within the academy; however, for purposes of this topic, degrees are secondary to educational content.

Advice and direction: true-life adventures. One important aspect of a good music school is that it is where a great many knowledgeable, often perceptive, sometimes insightful and almost always opinionated musicians are gathered in-one place. Honest opinions and feedback are very hard to come by in this business, but even harder once one has lost an institutionally mandated claim on these people's time and attention. Even while you have it, it is very hard to get your teachers or other mentors to give you their real opinions about your current work, your progress and your future; they will be afraid of hurting your feelings, or over praising and therefore "spoiling" you in some way, or encouraging you to do something which may prove to be wrong, or not encouraging you to do something which would have been right. Nevertheless, you have to armor yourself with the knowledge that any opinion about you can be wrong or right, and with the grains of salt which allow you not to be overly impressed by praise or discouraged by its opposite, and find benign ways to get people you respect to tell you, and to really hear, what they have to say.

You need this feedback because, certainly when you're young, you need more than your own ears to find out what your musical strengths are, the areas that need improvement, and how you fit in to the larger music community - that is, outside your school or department. **Ask advice.** It is more likely that someone will tell you that you might be stronger in different repertoire, or that you need to reinforce certain musical or technical areas, than that they will simply tell you that you're terrible, or wonderful. And this advice, when multiplied by a number of sources, can be immensely focusing and helpful.

Every musician needs to grow up with musical heroes, and with stories of adventures, good and bad, in the field. These can help you determine both who you want to be, and what kind of life you want to have. Stories are a serious part of your musical education, and you shouldn't leave school without a lot of them.

An edge. By the time you graduate - certainly from graduate education, but hopefully well before that - you will have acquired a knowledge of your own particular musical interests and strengths, and the skills to back them up, that will enable you to have a fighting chance out there in the world. School is an excellent place to affordably (given that you, or someone on your behalf, is already paying large sums for tuition) arm yourself with these skills and pursue your interests. Some possibilities are listed in the previous section, under "Related Skills and Flexibility."

Connections, and as a result, credibility. You shouldn't emerge from school without someone - or, preferably, many someones - who will be willing to make a phone call for you: to make an introduction, to get you past the tape round of an orchestra audition, to hook you up with someone who might be a musical partner. These people are the ones who will call because they believe in you, not because they are obligated to, as these are the recommendations which will carry some weight out in the world. They can include friends and colleagues as well as teachers; therefore, you should remember that you may be called upon to do as much for them, and that you should be more than willing to do so.

Providing all this should be included in the school's own, albeit unwritten, goals; however, getting this will be your responsibility: it is, in the end, your life and your career. There will be many items you can add to the above list, but thinking about what school can provide should begin with the question,

What do I need to succeed at my goals, that 1 could,
or should, be developing while at school?

Is this all there is?

Allen Hughes, former culture editor at The New York Times, used to tell a story about an interview he did with a young violinist. This young woman had the career which many of the readers of this book probably dream about; the 100 or so ideal engagements a year, playing in the world's finest halls and with the world's finest orchestras; a top manager; very good fees; the respect of the music community. And yet, she felt that her life had simply become a series of hotel rooms, and trying to remember whether she'd packed the hair dryer and what concerto she was performing that night. Though she still liked the actual playing, she was so unhappy with the life that it entailed that it was unclear how long her love of it would last. Her main reaction was, "There must be more to life than this."

A successful solo or chamber career is maintained not simply by an ability to keep playing well, but by a great tolerance for conditions that would not be tolerable for many of us. You have to like, or at least not mind, being on the road: living out of suitcases, rarely being home and maintaining a comparatively sketchy family life. You must be able to remain capable of smiling at those who are putting you up, picking you up at terminals, or entertaining you at a pre- or post-concert party, when you'd far rather be watching TV in your hotel room. And you must be able to concentrate and prepare for performance after long airplane flights or dealing with lost luggage. And on and on.

These conditions are worst, perhaps, during the period in which the career is taking off but not yet in the superstar league - which is, after all, the place where most quite successful careers stay. Though your income at that point may be very good, it has to be very good indeed to alleviate, on a regular basis, all the problems alluded to above. One of the artists interviewed about self-management said, "You have to want [a career] a lot to stand all the rejection you'll face..." We would amend that by adding, "and the life that comes with success, should you achieve it."

It is wise, therefore, to think about whether having this kind of career is worth the effort you'll put into getting it. There are many possible career configurations, based, for example, on a regional orientation, on using the university as a base, on developing a musical specialty for which there is a particular, but possibly limited, demand, even on developing a career in another field and performing on a limited basis. As you move along in your career, it is important to reflect regularly (and objectively, if you can) on where you want to go at a given point, and what the achievement of your goals will entail: on how realistic you are about achieving these goals, and what alternatives to your goals might be possible, would make you happy, and keep you in the field. You don't need to re-evaluate constantly, but you should do so periodically.

The Artist's Responsibility

It is a cliché of the music business these days that we're losing audiences – that the educated European immigrants who sustained the growth of many of the nation's musical organizations and events are dying off or moving to retirement communities, and that they've been replaced by a generation for whom the neglect of serious music education and changes in society's cultural values has resulted in an overall lack of interest in the kind of music most of you perform.

The situation isn't quite that simple, however. There are in fact a great many people listening to classical music, though the percentage, rather than the real numbers, who listen to it in concert halls may be shrinking. They're listening to it in different ways. They're listening to recordings, which get better all the time. They may be listening to the radio, watching musical performances on television, downloading music on their computers. And they're still coming out to hear live music, perhaps most enthusiastically at the summer festivals, on operatic stages, or at the highest profile events.

But the fact remains that for the performer seeking a career it is more and more important to take some responsibility for there being the possibility of careers for anyone at all in the future - that is, for there being an audience. You must actively be concerned with issues that for earlier generations, perhaps, could remain peripheral to their main performing activities, including education and even concert format; you must develop a unique and personal commitment to the future, not just the present or past, of your field.

Music, to be successful, must be participatory. The listener must feel some point of identification with the performance and/or the performer, to feel that for a time she is transported to another viewpoint, is experiencing the excitement of a new discovery or the replaying of a familiar and loved scenario. You must make sure this happens by shrinking the space between you and your listener (alluded to in the previous chapter) - which you achieve, first, by making sure that there is nothing in your musical or non-musical technique preventing your message from being heard, and then by being as truthful, focused and wonderful in your performance as it is possible to be.

It is nonetheless possible for your audience to be unable to really hear you for reasons that go beyond the scope of any individual recital. Unfamiliarity with the music, the people performing it and the situation in which it's performed is, sadly, the rule rather than the exception for most people these days. Therefore, a commitment to music education in the broadest sense must be part of your concerns as an artist. By this we don't mean telling people who Beethoven was, interesting as that might be: but, rather, to try to widen the circle of friends, to include more people in the family, the knowing and knowledgeable; to increase the number of those who aren't frightened by the concert hall or by music they haven't heard before; and to enlighten those who think that classical musicians are some strange breed, quite apart from normal humanity.

This may mean working on in-school performances, cultivating such opportunities and welcoming these engagements. It may also mean developing part of your performance which includes talking to the audience before the concert - or during it, if the situation is casual enough. It certainly means looking carefully at all aspects of performance, from finding people to bring into the halls and figuring out how to reach them to rethinking exactly what a concert is, what a concert hall is and when performances should be held. If you are producing your own concerts - if you have a chamber group that produces a series, for example - all these areas are directly in your control, and can be creatively explored for new solutions.

Whatever you do, though, should come out of your own experience as an artist, why you love music and why you want to share your music with others. You must learn to communicate why it's all worthwhile, and why it's even worth special effort. In articulating this to your public, you will first have to understand it yourself. Posing the question, and answering it with truth and with care, should remind you of the value of all that you are trying to achieve.

XIII. General Resources

Non-Profit Status

"Non-profit" (also called "not-for-profit") groups can receive contributions which are tax-deductible to the donor, and they are exempt from paying federal taxes, as well as certain state and city taxes. In order to be granted such status, the group has formally been incorporated as a not-for-profit corporation, and has been granted legal tax-exemption usually under section 501(c)(3) of the Internal Revenue Service code (there are other non-profit classifications for religious and educational organizations).

Being non-profit doesn't mean that no one makes any money; it means that money received by the group is used for fees, salaries, program expenses, administrative costs and the like, and not as profit to be distributed among principals of the organization (as profits might be among the shareholders or partners of a for-profit corporation, for example).

It is useful to have such status if your group does a significant amount of self-produced activity: puts on an annual concert series, organizes its own tours without fees or at fees which don't cover the expenses, commissions works, produces recordings, and more. However, it is something of a hassle to get, and, like any incorporation, there is a lot of formal organizing, paperwork and form-filing that will have to be complied with on a regular basis.

Volunteer Lawyers for the Arts (see below) can help you to understand the whole process, decide whether it would be important for you to have, and either do the legal work on your behalf or refer you to a lawyer who will.

If you go this route, you'll need some assistance in learning about the strange and constantly changing world of grants and funding. You can start by heading for your most local arts council, whether that's on the community, county, city or state level. They should be able to direct you to other sources of information, and to tell you what sort of groundwork you need to do before being of interest to funders.

There are many books on the subject, but talking to those who've done it, as well as to the funders themselves, is probably the best way to learn.

Volunteer Lawyers for the Arts
www.vlany.org
1 East 53rd Street, 6th Floor
New York, NY 10022
(212) 319-ARTS x 1

Founded in 1969, VLA was the first legal aid organization in the U. S. dedicated to providing free arts-related legal assistance to artists and arts organizations in all creative fields. It provides artists and arts organizations with limited pro bono legal advice, and helps to find further legal representation *on arts related issues* at affordable rates. Call to ask about eligibility for a free one hour consultation for individual artists or arts organizations. VLA also offers clinics, conferences and workshops on a variety of arts-related legal issues, has a speakers bureau, and operates a legal hotline for any artist or arts organization which needs quick answers to arts related legal questions. The hotline number is: 212-319-ARTS.

VLA publications include *All You Need to Know About the Music Business; The Musicians Business and Legal Guide; The Artist's Tax Guide and Financial Planner: How to Form Your Own New York Corporation;* and many other useful books.

Other help with the non-profit world, once you're in it:

If you would like to do some of your research about non-profits, grants, and various other ways that the arts and the rest of the world interact, try:

Americans for the Arts
www.artsusa.org
1 East 53rd Street
New York, NY 10022
(212) 223-2787

This organization both sells books for artists and arts organizations and maintains a library. Their publications catalog has lots of interesting items in it. ACA also keeps lists of grants and competitions.

Individual Artists Assistance (various):

New York Foundation for the Arts
www.nyfa.org
155 6th Avenue, 14th Floor
New York, NY 10013-1507
(212) 366-1778

NYFA is generally a very good, informed source of information about programs and assistance for individual artists. It can act as a non-profit conduit for individual artists' projects; has a very useful quarterly newsletter, FYI (though it's much more oriented to visual arts than music, and more to composers than performers even within the music field); administers a program of individual artist fellowships (again, for composers); runs a revolving loan program and a management services program for non-profit organizations.

Astral Artistic Services
www.astralartisticservices.org
230 South Broad Street, 3rd Floor
Philadelphia, PA 19102
(215) 735-6999

This organization was formed as a "pre-management resource center, providing ongoing assistance and advice free of charge [except for a nominal non-refundable application fee] to classical instrumentalists, singers, conductors and composers who are residing in the U. S." Certainly worth the application fee, if you can use any of the services which Astral provides: assistance with preparation of pr materials, grant applications and the like, advice on presentation and repertoire, translations, and more.

National Foundation for Advancement in the Arts (NFAA)
Astral Career Grants
www.artsawards.com/artprograms/astral.htm
800 Brickell Avenue, Suite 500
Miami, FL 33131
(800) 970-ARTS

No relationship to the previous Astral, these modest grants are awarded to meet expenses related to activities that will directly further an artists career. Examples of needs that qualify would be costs of travel to an audition, or repair of an instrument; examples of needs that would not qualify are medical expenses or general living support. The program is open to pianists, singers and composers, American citizens or full-time residents, and applicants must not be full-time students. Up to $250 grants are awarded at meetings held four times a year; no more than one grant a year can be given to one artist. Write for an application form.

Unions and Professional Associations

Here are the addresses of the two major musicians' unions:

American Federation of Musicians
www.afm.org
1501 Broadway, Suite 600 New York, NY 10036
(212) 869-1330

American Guild of Musical Artists (AGMA)
www.musicalartists.org
1430 Broadway, 14th Floor
New York, NY 10018
(212) 265-3687

Both of these organizations issue publications including important information about the field. The former has many more instrumentalists, the latter more singers, among its members. Union membership is required for much of the regular and free-lance work in most cities. Contact the above offices for the addresses and phone numbers of the local in your city, or look in the phone book.

There are several professional associations, organized by discipline, which serve as lobbyists for that part of the field and clearinghouses for information, and offer services of particular value to their constituencies. There is an Early Music America, several new music associations, and more. One example, of a particularly successful and useful professional association:

Chamber Music America
www.chambermusic.org
305 Seventh Avenue
New York, NY 10001
(212) 242-2022

CMA administers a number of grant programs for chamber groups, including one that helps ensembles establish residencies and one to commission chamber works. CMA produces an annual conference, runs workshops on career development and other important issues, offers technical assistance to its membership and publishes a newsletter, CMA Matters, a magazine, "Chamber Music, " and other publications relevant to the field of chamber music and chamber music education.

A professional association of a different kind:

College Music Society
www.music.org
312 East Pine Street
Missoula, MT 59802
(406) 721-9616

This organization offers several services of interest to musicians working within the academic community. Its members may attend conferences around the country, and may obtain special publications of interest to specific areas of the field - women's music, world music, etc. Both members and non-members may subscribe to a bi-monthly listing of music faculty openings nationwide.

Also, the CMS mailing lists are the most complete of any in this area of the field. Which leads to the question:

In addition to well-known sources of lists for musicians like Musical America, think creatively about where your constituency might overlap with another, though perhaps less obviously. For example, if you do cutting-edge music, perhaps a group which has mailing lists of people who go to cutting-edge dance would be more useful to you than a standard music list. In this case, it might be of interest to you to join an organization like:

Dance Theatre Workshop
www.dtw.org
219 W. 19th Street
New York, NY 10011
(212) 691-6500

Their members include composers as well as dancers, choreographers, and others, and members can get the benefits of bulk mail services, discounts on ads in the major newspapers, listings of rehearsal spaces, and an updated, interdisciplinary national press list. Be creative about finding out who and where your potential audience is, and how to get to them.

Some resources for composers:

Meet the Composer
www.meetthecomposer.org
Meet The Composer
75 Ninth Avenue, 3R Suite C
New York, NY 10011
(212) 645-6949

American Music Center
www.amc.net
30 West 26th Street
Suite 1001
New York, NY 10010-2011
(212) 366-5260

American Composers Forum
www.composersforum.org
332 Minnesota Street, Suite East 145
St. Paul, MN 55101-1300
(651) 228-1407

Some Final Resource Suggestions: Survival

Health Insurance

It would be wonderful to believe that by the time this book has been out for a short while this will be a non-issue, a universal health care package of some kind having been adopted nationally. Probably that won't be the case, and we will still have to muddle through for awhile. There is a publication which should be helpful: Health Insurance a Guide for Artists, Consultants, Entrepreneurs & Other Self-Employed, *by Lenore Janecek. It also covers retirement planning and other related issues. Also, check out*

The National Association for the Self-Employed
www.nase.org
P.O. Box 612067
DFW Airport
Dallas, TX 75261-2067
1-800-232-6273

Credit Union

Artists Community Federal Credit Union
www.artistscommunityfcu.org
351-A West 54 Street
New York, NY 10019
(212) 246-3344

This organization provides services that often are difficult for musicians to come by: loans for artistic purposes, lines of credit, and no-fee savings accounts and IRAs. It is a national organization. Call to learn how to join.

Day Jobs

Sometimes it does become necessary to support oneself by working a regular job, and earning a regular paycheck. It might be nice, though, to use your musical skills while doing this. Two publications which might help you to think about the various possibilities in the field other than playing or composing:

Careers in Music *is* a pamphlet available online (www.menc.org) by the Music Educators National Conference. Though very brief, it covers a lot of possibilities, and includes a list of sources to go to for further information.

Your Own Way in Music: A Career and Resource Guide, by Nancy Uscher, St. **Martins Press.** Vocational guidance. The most interesting parts of this book are the "case histories," which describe how highly trained musicians can be happy and fulfilled in various non-performance (and performance) jobs in the field. Ms. Uscher covers arts administration, acoustics, instrument making, free-lancing, academic positions, music therapy, Alexander technique teaching, copying, music production in all sorts of areas ... soup to nuts, in fact.

If you've decided to find a job in arts administration, there are several publications to which you can subscribe which may help you to find one:

Artsearch
www.tcg.org/artsearch
Theatre Communications Group, Inc.
520 Eighth Avenue 24th Floor
New York, NY 10018
(212) 609-5900

You can subscribe by mail or e-mail. Other possibilities are NYFA (listed earlier in this Chapter), APAP (www.artspresenters.org) and:

ArtJob
www.artjob.org
1743 Wazee Street, Suite 300
Denver, CO 80202
1-888-JOBS-232

ELLEN HIGHSTEIN

As Executive Director of Concert Artists Guild from 1986-1997, Ellen Highstein initiated and established a program of national concert presentations, a west coast office and music festival, a national program of radio residencies and broadcasts, the widely presented career development workshops, and a publications division, among other programs. She oversaw the growth of CAG's full service management to one of the nation's foremost non-profit managements, and CAG's annual International Competition to one of the largest and most respected in the country.

Prior to joining the CAG, Ms. Highstein was a music program officer at the New York State Council on the Arts, and continues to serve as a consultant for many government agencies and private foundations. As a writer, she has contributed articles to various magazines including *Chamber Music* magazine as well as to the *American Grove's,* and has collaborated on a workbook in theory for the Manhattan School of Music Preparatory Division.

Ms. Highstein holds degrees in composition from The Juilliard School and in education from New York University, has studied at the Paris Conservatory, and has trained and performed in piano, voice and conducting. She has been on the music department faculty of Brooklyn College Conservatory, and on the pre-college faculties of The Juilliard School and the Manhattan School of Music.

Ms. Highstein was appointed Director, Tanglewood Music Center, in November, 1997.

CONCERT ARTISTS GUILD

Concert Artists Guild is devoted to the career development of the emerging classical musician. Since 1951, CAG has advanced the careers of over 500 instrumentalists, singers, and ensembles from around the world. CAG's programs include the annual International Competition, the artist management program, commissions, fellowships, career development workshops, and publications. For information on Concert Artists Guild's programs, please write to: 850 Seventh Ave., Suite 1205, New York, NY 10019, or call: (212) 333-5200 or visit us on the Web at www.concertartists.org.